CONTENTS

CHAPTER ONE - THE MARKETING RESEARCH PROJECT 1

    Introduction 1
    Overview of the Project 1
    Benefits to be Gained 3
    Potential Problems 4
    Forming a Project Group 4
    Group Organization and Leadership 5
    Team Evaluation 6

    APPENDIX 1A - STUDENT BACKGROUND FORM 9
    APPENDIX 1B - TEAM INFORMATION SHEET 11
    APPENDIX 1C - PEER EVALUATION 13

CHAPTER TWO - MARKET SEGMENTATION AND POSITIONING STUDIES . 15

    A Typical Marketing Research Study 15
    Market Segmentation Studies 16
    Product Positioning Studies 17

CHAPTER THREE - CHOOSING A TOPIC AND WORKING WITH A CLIENT . 19

    Introduction 19
    Working with Campus Organization 19
    Working with Small Businesses 21
    Other Types of Clients 21
    Tips on Choosing a Topic 22
    Working With a Client 24
    You Are a Marketing Expert 25
    Managerial Decision Making and Marketing Research 26
    The Initial Meeting With Your Client 27

    APPENDIX 3A - CLIENT INTERVIEW FORM 33

CHAPTER FOUR - THE RESEARCH PROPOSAL 37

    Purpose of the Research Proposal 37
    Background Investigation 38
    Research Objectives 39
    Research Methodology 40
    Sampling Plan 45
    Data Gathering Instrument 47
    Data Collection 47
    Data Entry, Tabulation and Analysis 47
    Research Report 48
    Time and Cost Estimates 49
    Limitations 49

    APPENDIX 4A - ESTIMATED TIME LINE OF PROJECT ACTIVITIES 51
    APPENDIX 4B - RESEARCH PROPOSAL CHECKLIST 53

CHAPTER FIVE - QUESTIONNAIRE DESIGN 55

    From Objectives to Questions 55
    General Questionnaire Design Guidelines 56
    Question Form 58
    Closed-ended Questions 59
    Attitude Scaling 61
    Analysis Methods 64
    Questionnaire Mechanics 65
    Additional Considerations 68
    Precoding 69
    Pretest 71

    APPENDIX 5A - SAMPLE QUESTIONNAIRE 73

THE MARKETING RESEARCH PROJECT MANUAL

▼ ▼ ▼ ▼ ▼ ▼ ▼ ▼ ▼ ▼ ▼ ▼ ▼ ▼ ▼ ▼ ▼ ▼ ▼ ▼

Second Edition

Glen R. Jarboe
The University of Texas at Arlington

West Publishing Company

Minneapolis/St. Paul   ▼   New York   ▼   Los Angeles   ▼   San Francisco

WEST'S COMMITMENT TO THE ENVIRONMENT

In 1906, West Publishing Company began recycling materials left over from the production of books. This began a tradition of efficient and responsible use of resources. Today, up to 95% of our legal books and 70% of our college texts are printed on recycled, acid-free stock. West also recycles nearly 22 million pounds of scrap paper annually—the equivalent of 181,717 trees. Since the 1960s, West has devised ways to capture and recycle waste inks, solvents, oils, and vapors created in the printing process. We also recycle plastics of all kinds, wood, glass, corrugated cardboard, and batteries, and have eliminated the use of styrofoam book packaging. We at West are proud of the longevity and the scope of our commitment to our environment.

Production, Prepress, Printing and Binding by West Publishing Company.

CHAPTER SIX - SAMPLING AND SAMPLE SIZE DETERMINATION 77

    Introduction 77
    Census Versus Sample 77
    Probability Versus Nonprobability Samples 77
    Sampling from Lists 81
    Random Digit Dialing 83
    Intercept Interviewing 84
    Callback Procedures 85
    Additional Considerations in Choosing Sampling Methods 85
    Sample Size Determination 85

    APPENDIX 6A - CALL RECORD SHEET 89

CHAPTER SEVEN - DATA COLLECTION AND TABULATION 97

    Data Collection 97
    Coding 98
    Data Entry 99
    Computer Tabulation 101
    The SAS Program 102

    APPENDIX 7A - CODING SHEET FOR OPEN ENDED QUESTIONS 117
    APPENDIX 7B - SPSSX PROGRAMMING 125

CHAPTER EIGHT - DATA ANALYSIS 141

    Running SAS Procedures 141
    General Flow of Data Analysis 142
    The FREQUENCIES Procedure - One-way Distributions 142
    The MEANS Procedure - Simple Means 144
    The FREQUENCIES Procedure - Cross-tabulation 146
    The MEANS Procedure - Group Variables 153
    Simplifying Cross-tabulation Tables 154
    Choosing Cross-tabulations and Mean Breakdowns 158
    Constructing Split Variables 159
    Choosing the Appropriate Analysis Procedure 160

CHAPTER NINE - THE RESEARCH REPORT 161
    Overview of the Research Report 161
    Title Page 161
    Table of Contents 162
    Managerial Summary 163
    Background 163
    Objectives 163
    Research Design and Methodology 164
    Results 165
    Conclusions and Recommendations 176
    Limitations 178
    Appendices 179
    Oral Reports 179

CHAPTER TEN - MULTIVARIATE ANALYSIS 181

    Regression Analysis 181
    Discriminant Analysis 182
    Cluster Analysis 184
    Factor Analysis 185
    Analysis of Variance 187

CHAPTER ELEVEN - OTHER RESEARCH METHODOLOGIES 189

    Exploratory Research 189
    Descriptive Research 190
    Causal Research 193

PREFACE

This manual has been written to help you in conducting a student marketing research project. I have used a project of this type in teaching marketing research for many years and, on many occasions, my students have commented that they have found it to be one of their most rewarding educational experiences.

The project manual is designed to guide you, in a step-by-step manner, through a marketing research project. Your project will help you develop and refine a number of skills that can only be acquired by actually conducting marketing research. You will find that this manual will answer many detailed questions that students encounter while developing their project. Often, this type of detail is simply not covered in a marketing research textbook. The manual takes somewhat of a how-to-do-it approach. However, every student project is different and the purpose of the material presented in this manual is to encourage, not to restrain, your creativity.

This second edition of the project manual has been revised in a number of ways. A larger number and variety of research project examples have been provided to suggest the many different types of projects that you might undertake. The use of tear sheets has been continued and some, such as a checklist of the elements of the research proposal, have been added. The data analysis chapter has been expanded to further clarify the often-confusing problems of selecting and defining analysis variables.

A substantial improvement to the first edition is the provision of three data sets, each comprising 200 sample respondents which may be directly analyzed with the SAS and SPSS programs presented in chapters Seven and Eight. Data disks and descriptions of the various files they contain have been made available to the instructor. One of the three data sets was used to produce all of the computer output and numerical results reported in the project manual. Thus, using either the SAS or SPSS program, along with the data set, you should be able to produce the results contained in the manual, allowing you to gain valuable data analysis experience prior to analyzing the data from your own project. Two additional data sets will produce results similar, but not identical, to the results contained in the manual. The data disk also contains, in WORDPERFECT 5.1 format, the questionnaire contained in Chapter 5 as well as a copy of all of the various forms and tear sheets contained in the manual.

The manual has been designed around an example of a typical student project. The first few chapters orient you to the project and provide some useful information about finding and choosing a client to work with. In Chapter Three, you will meet Ms. Allen, the proprietor of Apex Dry Cleaning, as a group of student consultants interview her to determine how they can be of assistance. In Chapter Four, you will see how the information from this interview is used develop research objectives and prepare a research proposal. In Chapter Five, you will learn how the objectives in the proposal are translated into an actual questionnaire. Chapter Six will help you in choosing a sampling method and provide you some help in designing sampling plans and procedures.

Chapter Seven will show you how to get the survey data into the computer and will provide you an introduction to two software programs commonly used for tabulating data, SAS (Statistical Analysis System) and SPSS (Statistical Package for the Social Sciences). Independent discussions will be provided for each program so that you will be able to use either with little reference to the discussion of the other. Computer programs, for both SAS and SPSS, are provided to accompany the Apex Dry Cleaners questionnaire.

Chapter Eight introduces some of the most commonly used tabulation procedures; frequency distributions and cross-tabulations. It also discusses how to use some of the basic statistical summary measures discussed in your textbook. Chapter Nine will help you prepare a research report. It will show you how to analyze results and translate them into findings, conclusions and recommendation.

Chapter Ten provides a brief overview of several sophisticated multivariate analysis techniques and includes some typical computer statements for using these techniques in either SAS or SPSS. The final chapter shows you how the skills you have acquired in doing your projects can be applied to other types of marketing research studies.

I believe that you will find this project to be a genuinely rewarding educational experience. You will not only be acquiring and applying new skills, but you will be challenged to think like a marketer. You will also experience, firsthand, the excitement of a career in marketing, whether as a supplier or as a user of marketing research.

It is my hope that this manual has not left too many of your questions unanswered. Good luck!

Glen Jarboe
The University of Texas at Arlington
November, 1992

CHAPTER ONE
THE MARKETING RESEARCH PROJECT

INTRODUCTION

This manual has been written to help guide you through the conduct of a marketing research project. It will require you to use the marketing research process to solve a marketing problem from problem definition to final report. This manual is intended to answer many of the questions that are typically encountered in translating the concepts and ideas you have learned into practical application. It is not likely to answer all your questions. However, it will discuss most of the difficulties that students have encountered in conducting projects of this type.

This manual is intended only as a guide. While it has somewhat of a "how to do it" focus, you will find that you must exercise considerable creativity and originality in applying your ideas. You will encounter many questions to which there is no single correct answer. No two researchers or research groups will approach a problem in exactly the same way. Every marketing research project is unique. However, you and your classmates working on different projects may encounter many of the same situations and this manual has been written to address them.

OVERVIEW OF THE PROJECT

You will be completing an entire marketing research project from start to finish. As discussed in your textbook, such a project involves a series of steps that begins with the identification of a research problem and ends with a final report of findings, conclusions, and recommendations. An overview of this process is included in your textbook, and a typical diagram of it is contained in Figure 1.1. You should note that the steps involve,

FIGURE 1.1
The Marketing Research Process

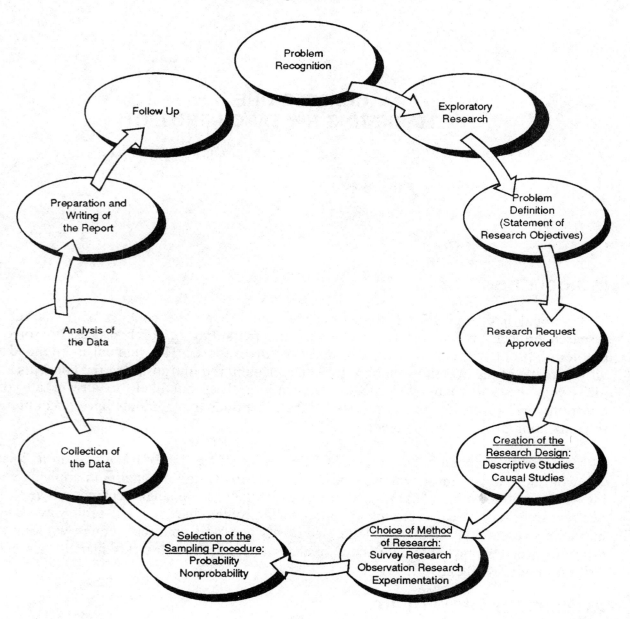

among other things, the specification of a target population, the development of a method for sampling from this group, and the development of a questionnaire. The process will also involve entering the data into the computer, running programs to generate tabulations, and analyzing and interpreting these tabulations. Chapters in your textbook and lecture material address each of these aspects of the research process.

Throughout the conduct of this project, your instructor will serve as an advisor to answer questions not covered in this manual. However, this is *your* project. All of the important steps will be carried out by you and your group. In effect, your team may be thought of as a group of student consultants and, throughout the term, you will be working for a "client," some organization to which you believe you can be of assistance. Your instructor will probably allow you to develop your own list of potential clients and select one of them to work with. If you have difficulty coming up with a client, your instructor may have some ideas. Business people often contact universities with ideas for student projects, and your instructor may know of some. However, the author's experience has been that most student groups can come up with several excellent project ideas without much prompting.

In effect, your student group becomes a small marketing research company. You will gain an appreciation for the value and conduct of marketing research and develop some feeling about this field as a potential career opportunity. While this process will represent a lot of hard work, students often report that it is one of their most satisfying experiences in business school.

BENEFITS TO BE GAINED

Practical Experience. The most obvious benefit to be gained from conducting this project is the practical experience you will acquire. Many students find that they do not truly understand the concepts and ideas they learn in the classroom until they are required to apply them in an actual situation. Such a fundamental concept as market segmentation takes on a new meaning when you are required to carefully identify, define, and measure the characteristics of some important customer group(s).

Satisfaction of Producing a Product. Students often find considerable satisfaction in doing the marketing research project. This exercise will involve you from start to finish in solving a practical problem. At this point, it may be hard for you to imagine what the final product will be like. However, if your feelings at the end of the term are similar to those of other students, you will be proud to see what you have done when the study has been completed. The final report of your project will truly be a product that you and your research group have created.

Application of Skills. This project will require you to apply a variety of skills. Some of these skills may be entirely new, such as designing a questionnaire or using a PC and a computer program to tabulate data. Others may be skills that you began to acquire in other classes but have not applied to marketing problems, for example, using the graphics capabilities of a spreadsheet program to prepare graphs or bar charts.

Exposure to a Professional Experience. You may find that this project is as close as you will come during your college career to experiencing the things that professionals regularly encounter. A single course in marketing research is not going to make you a professional marketing researcher. In fact, some universities are beginning to offer entire programs of study for that purpose. Such a program would expand a number of chapters in your textbook into entire courses, for example, questionnaire design, sampling, or data collection. However, the process you experience will be substantially the same. If you aspire to a career as a marketing researcher, you will get the opportunity to experience firsthand the things marketing researchers do. If your career takes you into marketing management, you should benefit significantly through your understanding of the kinds of problems that marketing research can (and can't) help solve, and provide you an increased sensitivity to the difficulty of conducting high-quality research.

In addition, you may find your final report very useful when you begin looking for a career. Most recruiters, while they may not ask for it, are pleased to see examples of your college work. Your transcript tells them something about the things that you should *know* as a result of the university experience. Projects of this type help them to evaluate the things that you can *do*.

POTENTIAL PROBLEMS

Difficulty of Working with Others. While the benefits of doing this project may be substantial, do not underestimate its difficulty. While some people are naturally attracted to working on projects as part of a group, others take a more independent approach to their education. A project of this type will require you to work with and depend upon others, some of whom may not share your level of knowledge and enthusiasm. This is an excellent opportunity to experience the dynamics of working as part of a team.

Staying on Schedule. The most difficult aspect of this project for many groups of students is adhering to a schedule that will ensure that the project is completed on time. As illustrated by the outline of the research process, many of the steps must be performed sequentially (e.g. you cannot begin to gather data until the questionnaire is designed and the sampling plan is prepared). Students often find that it is difficult to complete their projects within one term and delays and procrastination will seriously affect your final product. Your ultimate goal is to produce a research report of high quality and, as far as your client is concerned, the final report is your product. No matter how good a job you do in each of the previous phases of the research project, if your final report is poorly written or does not reflect a thorough analysis of the data, much of your hard work may be for naught, and this may be reflected in your final grade. As a general guideline, try to have all of your data gathered three or four weeks prior to the end of the term. This should leave you with adequate time for data analysis and report writing.

FORMING A PROJECT GROUP

Your instructor may simply assign you to a project group without regard to your preferences. However, it is likely that he or she may allow you some discretion in deciding with whom you want to work. Typically, a group size of five to seven works well. In order to allow you to focus on the important tasks of research design and analysis, your instructor may expect each student to conduct only a small number of interviews, perhaps twenty or twenty-five. Consequently, groups smaller than five may generate inadequate sample sizes. In larger groups, it may be difficult to ensure the adequate involvement of all the team members. It may also be difficult to reach a consensus on important research design issues.

There are a number of things that you might consider in forming a project group.

1.   It would be desirable to have more than one person who has some experience with a word processor. Preferably they would both use the same program, such as WORDPERFECT or MICROSOFT WORD.

   (*Author's Note: This entire manual was prepared with WORDPERFECT 5.1 using Times Roman and Helvetica fonts*)

2.   It would also be desirable to have one or two people who enjoy using the computer. The SAS and SPSS programs are easy to learn, even for those with limited computer experience. However, the process is facilitated if one already has a working knowledge of how to use the campus computer facilities. In addition, it would be useful to have a group member who knows how to use (or wants to learn more about) the graphics capability of the PC. This would enhance the appearance and quality of your final report.

3.   It is easier for students with similar class schedules to get together for meetings. Some groups may try to include members who live close to school. In a large metropolitan area, students who live in close proximity to each other might want to get together.

4.   Some people naturally seek others with whom they feel they can work compatibly, perhaps based upon a previous group experience in another class. This may be an important factor so long as consideration is given to the skills mentioned above.

Appendix 1A contains a brief information sheet that your instructor may ask you to turn in. If some people desire to form their own work group, the sheets should be turned in together. This information sheet will help the instructor to check on the skills inventory in each group or to form groups of students who do not express any membership preferences.

GROUP ORGANIZATION AND LEADERSHIP

On the day when group assignments are made, your instructor may allow you to use the last few minutes of the class period to get together, exchange phone numbers, and plan for your first meeting (the form contained in Appendix 1B provides you a place to record team names, phone numbers, meeting times, etc.). Prior to your first meeting, every member of the group should review this manual to get an idea of what will be involved in the project. At least the first three chapters should be read entirely. Reading the entire project manual would be even more desirable (it isn't all that long, you are going to have to do it sooner or later, and it will give you a better idea of what the course and project are about).

At your first meeting you should appoint (or elect) a team leader and have him or her make this known to the instructor. It will be up to the group to decide on the limits of this person's authority. Optimally, all group decisions will be made by consensus, and this person will simply be the instructor's primary point of contact with the group. However, occasional disputes may arise that will have to be resolved. The group might decide that all such questions will be voted on, or perhaps the group leader will be allowed to resolve them.

One of the most difficult aspects of group projects is getting the entire group together on short notice. It may be desirable to establish a regularly scheduled weekly meeting, for instance, Wednesday afternoon at 3:00 as well as one or two alternative meeting times (some project activities require group meetings more than once a week). The group (or team leader) may occasionally decide to cancel a weekly meeting if it is not needed. However, having a preplanned, regular meeting time will allow each group member to schedule other activities around the expected meeting.

Each member of the group should plan to attend all regularly scheduled meetings. This will help to maintain everyone's involvement. It will also ensure that the benefits of group, rather than individual, effort are realized. This is especially important in the early problem-formulation and questionnaire-design phases, as well as in the later analysis and report phases. At the end of each meeting, the activities for the next group meeting should be discussed so that all group members will be prepared.

Some groups try to overcompartmentalize this project. For instance, they will assign one group member to write a section of the research proposal or a few specific questions of the questionnaire. While this may be a useful way to prepare for meetings, the proposal or questionnaire will require a high level of group involvement to ensure that all of its parts are consistent. Stringing together several paragraphs, each written by a different person without regard to the other parts of a research proposal, is almost certain to result in project design that is inconsistent and unworkable. Having each team member write a few of the questions for a questionnaire may result in a survey instrument that is unprofessional and does not flow smoothly.

TEAM EVALUATION

At the end of the term, your instructor may ask you to evaluate the contribution of the members of your group to the project. The instructor may provide you a form or suggest that you use the one contained in Appendix 1C. The form in the appendix requests that you evaluate only the other members of your group. However, you may use the comments section to point out various aspects of your own performance. Often, the instructor will choose to assign an overall grade to the group project and then give separate grades to each individual group member. This would reward some team members for their extra hard work and creativity.

APPENDIX 1A
MARKETING RESEARCH PROJECT - STUDENT BACKGROUND FORM

NAME _____ Team _____

CLASSIFICATION   Freshman   Sophomore   Junior   Senior Graduate

MAJOR   Marketing   Other Business   Other

RESIDENCE   On Campus Near Campus Far from Campus

EMPLOYMENT   None   Part Time Full Time

ARE MOST OF YOUR CLASSES   Day Night

FOUNDATION COURSES COMPLETED

Consumer Behavior	No	Yes
Psychology	No	Yes
Marketing Strategy	No	Yes
Information Systems/Management Science	No	Yes
At least one semester of Statistics	No	Yes
OTHER_____	No	Yes
OTHER_____	No	Yes

COMPUTER LANGUAGES YOU HAVE USED

BASIC, FORTRAN, or COBOL	No	Yes
SAS -Statistical Analysis System	No	Yes
SPSS - Statist. Package for the Social Sciences . .	No	Yes
Other_____		Yes

OTHER COMPUTER SKILLS

Word Processing	No	Yes
Spreadsheets	No	Yes
Graphics Programs	No	Yes
Other_____		Yes
Other_____		Yes

Have you used a personal computer and modem to
communicate with campus computers? . . . .   No   Yes

Have you performed a survey research project in
any other course? . . . .   No   Yes

Other Information Desired by the Instructor:

_____

_____

_____

APPENDIX 1B
MARKETING RESEARCH PROJECT - TEAM INFORMATION SHEET

YOUR NAME_____ Team _____

MEETING TIMES: DAY   TIME   PLACE

      Regular Meeting   _____   _____   _____

      Alternate # 1   _____   _____   _____

      Alternate # 2   _____   _____   _____

GROUP COMPOSITION:

TEAM MEMBER_____ Phone_____

Special Skills _____

TEAM MEMBER_____ Phone_____

Special Skills _____

TEAM MEMBER_____ Phone_____

Special Skills _____

TEAM MEMBER_____ Phone_____

Special Skills _____

TEAM MEMBER_____ Phone_____

Special Skills _____

TEAM MEMBER_____ Phone_____

Special Skills _____

TEAM MEMBER_____ Phone_____

Special Skills _____

APPENDIX 1C
MARKETING RESEARCH PROJECT - PEER EVALUATION

The purpose of this form is to allow you to evaluate the relative contribution of the members of your group to the project you have performed. Your instructor may ask you to assign a score to the overall contribution of each team member or she/he may ask you to evaluate individual areas as well as the overall contribution. In making your evaluation, you should divide 100 points among the members of the group, **other than yourself.** Thus, the total in each column should be 100. You will not evaluate yourself. However, you may use the "Comments" space at the bottom of the form, as well as the back, to mention specific aspects of your performance, or to provide written comments about the team members.

TEAM MEMBERS	SPECIAL AREAS			OVERALL CONTRIBUTION
	CONCEPTU-ALIZATION	PROJECT EXECUTION	OTHER	
Your Name:	DO NOT EVALUATE YOURSELF			------ ------
Other Team Members:				
TOTAL	100	100	100	100

COMMENTS:

13

CHAPTER TWO
MARKET SEGMENTATION AND POSITIONING STUDIES

A TYPICAL MARKETING RESEARCH STUDY

In this course, you will learn that there are a large number of ways that marketing research may be applied in solving management problems. For instance, exploratory research, such as focus group interviews, may be used to help management better define problems or opportunities. Observational studies may be used to monitor consumer behavior in an unobtrusive way. Concept tests, copy tests, product usage tests, and test markets are all examples of marketing research studies that can enhance the quality of managerial decision making. Throughout a career in marketing research, an account executive might develop an expertise in all of these areas, as well as others.

At first, it might seem that any type of research study could be used as a vehicle for a group research project in a marketing research class. However, many of the marketing research studies mentioned above would be inappropriate. They might require too much time and expertise, or they might expose you to only a small subset of the skills that could be developed through other projects. In the concluding chapter of this manual we will briefly discuss some of these other types of projects and illustrate how your newly acquired experience might help you in performing more sophisticated tasks.

This project manual is oriented toward the performance of a market segmentation and/or positioning study, a type of project that has proven very useful and doable throughout the author's years of teaching the marketing research course. It provides students with a rewarding and practical exposure to marketing research. Some reasons for this are:

1.   Knowledge and abilities gained in a segmentation and/or positioning study are likely to be applicable to other types of marketing research.

2.   Nearly any type of organization (manufacturer, service business, nonprofit organization, or club) that provides a product or service to a group of constituents (customers, contributors, benefactors,   club members) could benefit from such a study.

3.   Often, this would be one of the first types of studies performed by an organization that has not previously used marketing research.

4.   The performance of a segmentation and/or positioning study requires a wide variety of skills, such as questionnaire design, statistical analysis, computer usage and report writing.

MARKET SEGMENTATION STUDIES

Since you have taken at least one marketing course, it should be apparent that market segmentation is one of the fundamental concepts of modern marketing. Nearly all markets are segmented; try to think of one that isn't. Even something as mundane as salt is segmented by the way it is used. There is a considerable difference between the little individual serving packets and a manufacturer who adds several pounds at a time in making a food product. Think of any product you buy or all the stores where you shop. You should be able to see at least a few similarities between yourself and others who buy the same product or shop at the same store. You might also see considerable differences between your segment and other segments who buy different products or shop at different stores. Such differences can be extremely important, and valuable, to the marketing manager.

The marketing concept suggests that the consumer should be the focus of marketing strategy, planning, and decision making. Since it is obvious that human beings are not all alike, it would be illogical to offer one marketing strategy to all consumers on a take-it-or-leave-it basis. The extreme alternative to this, a custom-designed marketing strategy for each customer, would also be impractical. Market segmentation offers a happy medium.

Ideally, the marketing manager can find enough uniformity among large groups of consumers that, by designing a strategy tailored to the group, the needs of individuals within the group will be substantially satisfied. Quite often, new product opportunities are suggested when it is discovered that the needs of some subgroup of consumers are not being adequately met. Sometimes, potential new distribution strategies are revealed when the preferred shopping behavior of consumers is found to be inconsistent with the stores that currently sell the product. Some consumers are found to be especially price sensitive and may be reached with a more basic and less expensive model of the product. Or perhaps some group of consumers who would be expected to have a natural desire for the product are not being reached with the current promotional strategies. Alternative messages or media may be suggested.

Thus, products or services are directed at some well-defined market segment. On one hand, the product or service may have been specifically designed to meet some unsatisfied need. In other cases, a good idea was first discovered, and then the manager may have searched for groups to whom the idea would be especially attractive. In either case, a higher level of sales and profitability are likely to be realized with a segmented strategy. Even after a new product is launched or a new service is offered, segmentation remains important. Multibillion-dollar companies continue to conduct annual market segmentation studies at a cost of hundreds of thousands of dollars to track changes in market segments and discover the emergence of new ones.

Market segmentation studies are able to provide answers to some of the most basic types of questions asked by marketing managers. For example:

1. Who buys my product and what characteristics do they have in common?

2. Who doesn't buy my product?

3. How much of the purchasing of my product is done by consumers who are especially heavy purchasers? Should I treat them differently?

4. Are my brand-loyal customers different in some way from those who only buy my brand occasionally or not at all?

5. Which groups of consumers are generally aware (or unaware) of the existence of my product, service, or store?

6. Do the people who have tried my product at least one time differ from those who have never tried it?

7. Should I try to use one marketing strategy to reach all my potential customers, or might I need two separate marketing plans?

A market segmentation study may be used to provide useful answers to these and a wide variety of other questions of genuine interest to managers, the extent of which is only limited by the ingenuity and imagination of the manager and the research designer.

PRODUCT POSITIONING STUDIES

Another important type of marketing research project is a product positioning study. This type of study could be carried out as a separate marketing research project. However, because it shares many things in common with the segmentation study, the two are often combined.

Product positioning studies are designed to determine how present and potential customers perceive the firm's products or services compared to those of competitors. Marketing managers often talk of a product's position or of the desire to reposition a product. They may also attempt to investigate consumer needs and desires for current products or for new product offerings. Managers are interested in exploring what unfilled product positions might exist within the market of interest.

Product positioning studies are sometimes referred to as image studies. Psychological theory suggests that people respond to things according to the way they *perceive* them, which may be inconsistent with the way they really *are*. Even if the firm has the highest-quality product on the market (as measured by objective testing), this would not provide a motive for purchasing unless consumers *believe* that the product is of high quality. Another potential problem for the marketing manager is that even if consumers believe the product to be of high quality, it may not provide a strong purchase motive if consumers do not see its best attributes as being important. Thus, in a positioning study, you will probably be interested in both consumer beliefs about products as well as the importance they place on each product characteristic.

A common mistake sometimes made by naive marketing managers is to assume that they know how consumers perceive the product. Many marketing managers may have little direct contact with the target market. Thus, the product positioning study is designed to help the manager view her or his own product through the eyes of the typical consumer. Brand managers spend most of their professional lives intensely interested in a single product, and this can create a very biased view of the consumer's desires. The results of a product positioning study may confirm the manager's preexisting opinions or may be a source of considerable disappointment.

Product or service perceptions may not be common across all possible groups of customers. Sometimes two groups of customers may perceive the firm's offering differently. For instance, consider a product such as the beverage Tang. Some customers may consider it a tasty substitute for orange juice in the morning, while others see it as a convenient afternoon snack for their children. And even if customer perceptions are similar, all groups may not desire a product positioned in a certain way. For instance, most automobile buyers are likely to perceive a Mercedes as a high-priced luxury automobile, but all do not prefer Mercedes as a possible purchase.

The term positioning provides additional clues as to how such a study would be carried out. You may think of the word *position* as a geometric concept, that is, a point in space. If so, you should also recognize that most positions have importance with respect to other positions. In other words, it might not be particularly revealing to know what the product's image is among consumers unless we also know the image of other products to provide a basis for comparison. These other products could include those of competitors as well as products the consumer believes to be ideal.

CHAPTER THREE
CHOOSING A TOPIC AND WORKING WITH A CLIENT

INTRODUCTION

Your first assignment involves the submission of one or more project ideas to your instructor. Your instructor will try to help you choose the most interesting and/or doable project. The submission of your project ideas can be as simple as listing some things of interest to the members of the group. Examples might include:

A study to help increase business at Bob's Pizza.

A study to evaluate the quality of on-campus food service.

A study of student perceptions of the Marketing Club.

In your first group meeting, you should probably try to come up with a list of possible "clients." Generating several project ideas should not be difficult. Any organization that has a group of customers to serve is a candidate. There will probably be several people in your group who own or work in a business, or know someone who does. If you are interested in working with a business, it is probably best to stick with a small one. While a large company may admire your enthusiasm, it is likely that it has research resources of its own.

WORKING WITH CAMPUS ORGANIZATIONS

Obvious sources of "clients" are campus organizations and services, since few would have a budget for marketing research. These could include:

1.   Campus clubs and organizations such as fraternities, sororities, professional organizations such as the AMA, and intramural sports. Such organizations may have many unanswered questions regarding their members and/or prospective members such as activities preferred, interesting guest speakers and how to attract additional members.

2.   Campus business services such as dining, food services, the movie theater, the book store, and the campus newspaper. In many ways, these organizations operate as small businesses and experience many of the very same problems. A research study could be used to measure customer perceptions and satisfaction and to evaluate ways to increase revenues and profitability.

3.   Other campus services such as the health center, the counseling and testing service, the student activities office, the police force, and parking administrators. Even though profitability may not be the ultimate goal of these organizations, by serving a group of constituents (customers), they experience many of the same problems of business organizations. Because profitability is often not their objective, studies of customer satisfaction may take on special importance for these types of organizations.

4.   Organizers of campus activities such as bicycle races, flea markets, and Greek Week. The development of a single program or activity may require a host of important decisions. When should the event be held? What time of day? Where? Who would want to participate and how should we reach them? A marketing research study could be invaluable in helping to make such decisions and in contributing to the success of the event.

During a spring semester, the student marketing club conducted a survey to determine student attitudes toward campus organizations, most likely sources of information and attitudes towards various activities that might stimulate student interest. The results of the survey were used to plan the recruiting effort during the following fall semester. Club activities were chosen to reflect student interests and these activities were featured in advertisements designed and placed so as to reach the most likely prospective members. The club leadership felt that the results of the survey contributed to an especially successful recruiting effort.

WORKING WITH SMALL BUSINESSES

Some groups prefer to work with an area business. While the experience may be little different from working with a campus organization, students sometimes feel that this type of project is closer to the "real world." Small businesses often do not have adequate budgets for marketing research. Some may be unaware of its potential benefits. Others may have made a subjective judgment that the value of commercial marketing research is not likely to exceed its cost. (See your text for a discussion of the value and cost of marketing research) However, most managers who are concerned with satisfying their customers or increasing their revenues can intuitively see the value in obtaining additional information from outside sources. Given that this project will be offered at little or no charge, small businesses often make enthusiastic clients.

It should be easy to come up with a list of interesting clients. A drive down any commercial street will reveal a host of possibilities. Restaurants, hair stylists, dance studios, bookstores, dry cleaners, and computer stores are all potential clients. The managers of most of these establishments would readily admit that there would be value in knowing more about their present and potential customers.

> In a study of preferences and patronage at a mexican food cafeteria, respondents were interviewed while standing in line waiting to be served. As an incentive and show of appreciation, respondents were offered a free desert for each member of their party. In fact, several non-desert eaters turned down the opportunity, many remarking that the they found the study to be interesting and/or that they were glad to contribute to the student's study. The results of the study prompted several changes in menu selection, pricing and the general operation of the business.

OTHER TYPES OF CLIENTS

Occasionally, students have performed research projects on behalf of the local city government. For example, one particularly interesting project studied community reactions to the rapid growth that the city was experiencing. It also presented the respondents with a number of either-or choices with regard to the allocation of the city's limited resources. In another project, students worked with the planning department of a large city to study efforts to revitalize a run-down and economically disadvantaged area.

The local city government of a rapidly growing city of around 250,000 called on a group of students to study community attitudes towards the rapid growth that the city had experienced over the previous several years. A telephone survey using random digit dialing was utilized to conduct a random sample of 300 households. The study addressed many issues involving growth problems and requested that respondents rank order their priorities regarding the allocation of limited tax revenues. The questionnaire was kept brief by utilizing a dichotomous response format for most of the questions. Although it was possible to complete the questionnaire in less than five minutes, the student interviewers noted that many interviews were much longer due to the respondent's desire to amplify their responses. City officials reported that the results of the study were invaluable in providing a "customer" perspective on the operation of city government.

TIPS ON CHOOSING A TOPIC

It may take two or more group meetings for your group to decide upon a project. The first meeting could involve a discussion of the interests of the various group members and a brainstorming session to generate a list of prospective clients. After contacting these clients, another meeting can be held to discuss the interest of prospective clients and to decide on a project.

Chapter Four will discuss the research proposal and will suggest a number of decisions that must be made in choosing a research design. However, at this point, it will be useful for you to consider some possible complications that might increase the difficulty of completing your project.

1.   Avoid low-incidence product or service categories. For instance, a study of consumer satisfaction with digital audio tape could be very difficult if it is necessary to call fifty people to find each qualified respondent.

A group of students was interested in studying peoples' attitudes toward a new recording technology, digital audio tape. Their intention was to compare the attitudes of owners and non-owners of the equipment by interviewing fifty people from each group. They chose telephone interviewing as the most desirable method of gathering data and random digit dialing to reach members of each group. About one-third of the people contacted were willing to participate in the interview. After making approximately 150 telephone calls, they had located 50 people who had not purchased the new tape machines and only four who had. At this point, the students estimated that they would have to make about 1350 additional telephone contacts to find 50 buyers of the machines. Fortunately, an understanding instructor allowed them to modify the goals of the study.

2.   It is easier to measure the satisfaction of existing customers than to discover the motives of noncustomers. Often, present customers can be surveyed through a brief interview on the client's premises. Noncustomers would have to be contacted by other means. In this case, the low-incidence caution described above may become important.

An owner of a sit-down family restaurant was interested in current customer opinions of menu selection and quality. No listing of names and addresses of customers was available and it was considered inappropriate to interview customers during their dining experience. After clearly explaining to management the potential biases associated with respondent willingness to participate, a sampling method was developed. As an inducement to participate in the study, customers were asked to leave their name and telephone number on a small card if they were willing to be called at home to be interviewed. In return, they would be mailed a coupon offering them $3.00 off on their next restaurant visit. Within one week, the students, had obtained sufficient names to complete 120 interviews. Of the possible respondents who filled out the card, over 80 percent agreed to be interviewed when called.

3.   Avoid projects that call for respondents to give opinions about which they have little knowledge. For instance, it might be difficult for randomly selected respondents to give opinions about the capabilities of high performance sports cars.

4.   Some projects require respondents to answer questions on sensitive or embarrassing topics. These types of projects may require special care in their design. Many respondents may be reluctant to participate and, among those who do, the responses may be subject to considerable response bias.

A group of students decided to help the owner of a local home security business, who was interested in people's attitudes toward home security systems and what measures people may have taken (or would like to take), to increase their home security. The students submitted the idea to the instructor who suggested that most homeowners might be rather skeptical of someone calling them or coming to their door to ask them about their security measures. The students solved the problem by approaching the local police force who became interested in the results of the study. Consequently, the police department provided the students a letter introducing them and briefly describing its interest in the results of their project. A police department telephone number was also provided where the respondents might call to further verify the student's authenticity. The project was very successful.

WORKING WITH A CLIENT

Remember, you should think of your project team as a group of marketing consultants working to provide a marketing research study to a client. The initial contact should probably be made by one or two group members. During this conversation, there are several things that you should make very clear:

1.   The project will be performed by a group of student consultants taking an introductory course in marketing research. Your instructor may provide you some assistance by answering your questions and reviewing your work. However, his or her limited involvement will not ensure that you do not make mistakes or that your project would be up to industry standards.

2.   The project will involve survey research using a formal questionnaire. If the client has something else in mind, such as a focus group or a project involving only secondary data gathering, this would not meet your course requirements.

3.   The project will not take a great deal of the client's time. His or her involvement could be limited to:

   a.   One or two meetings of an hour or so in duration to gather background material about the client's organization, marketing strategies, information needs, and potential marketing decisions.

   b.   Occasional phone calls or visits to report on the progress of the study and/or to clear up areas of confusion.

   c.   The review and approval of your research proposal and questionnaire.

   d.   Providing background data, such as industry trade publications or published research reports.

4.   The project may deviate considerably from what might be provided by a professional marketing research organization. The sample will be relatively small and the questionnaire limited in length and scope.

5.   Because the project is not being conducted by professional researchers, the results should be interpreted with caution, especially if used as a basis for marketing strategy planning or decision making.

6.   If you are not prepared to make a commitment to the client during your initial cold call, make sure that she or he understands that the choice of a client to work with will be made by your project group with the advice of your instructor. After this decision is made, you will notify him or her.

YOU ARE A MARKETING EXPERT

Perhaps one of the most attractive aspects of a career in marketing research is that it forces an individual to become familiar with a variety of different areas of business. An account executive in a custom marketing research company could, in a given year, study fifteen to twenty different products or services and be involved in different stages of many projects at the same time. Considering the diversity of so many different types of businesses, one might wonder how people could develop an expertise in every possible field. The answer is, they usually don't.

Rather, the capable marketing researcher develops a feel for common problems and solutions without getting lost in the detail that often obscures these problems from management. The one area in which a good marketing researcher or consultant *does* become an expert is general marketing. The researcher develops an intuitive feel for marketing management and decision making as a process.

MANAGERIAL DECISION MAKING AND MARKETING RESEARCH

Before discussing how the researcher can help the marketing manager, we will examine what managers do. The essence of management is decision making; managers make decisions with respect to the allocation of resources. Marketing managers deal with special kinds of business resources. These are the controllable marketing variables, usually referred to as the marketing mix. They may have been referred to in your Principles of Marketing textbook as "the four P's." Marketing managers try to allocate these resources in the most efficient manner by directing them towards specific market segments.

Any decision involves a choice from a set of alternatives. The existence of two or more alternatives, one of which is believed to be more desirable, is the basis for decision making. In evaluating the desirability of alternatives, the manager must attempt to predict the outcomes resulting from alternative choices. This can be especially difficult since these outcomes will not occur until sometime in the future, and they may be affected by a wide variety of factors that are out of the manager's control. Nevertheless, the manager must gather as much information as reasonably possible to make an accurate prediction of these outcomes.

The information that the manager will use to predict these outcomes could come from a variety of sources, such as his or her own background and experience, the internal records of the company, information purchased from syndicated data services, or library research. However, sometimes the information is simply not available from any source and must be gathered directly. Such is the case with primary research studies.

A very useful type of information involves consumer response. Below is a brief list of some of the types of consumer response questions that might be asked by a typical marketing manager:

1. How would my customers react if I raised or lowered my price by five percent? What if my competitors did the same?

2. What would have a more positive impact on my sales, a five percent price reduction or the addition of a more attractive product feature?

3. How would my business be affected if I moved to a more desirable location?

4. Should I increase my advertising budget? For each dollar of increased advertising, how much additional revenue would be generated?

5. Should I add additional styles and colors to my product line?

Clearly the answers to questions such as these will affect the decision of the manager. Even prior to conducting marketing research, the manager probably has tentative answers based upon his or her own background and experience. The manager also knows that there may be considerable cost incurred if these beliefs are wrong. Thus, marketing research can substantially reduce the inherent risk in decision making. It can do this by providing the manager with an additional and valuable perspective, that of the actual consumer.

THE INITIAL MEETING WITH YOUR CLIENT

Using a managerial decision-making perspective will help you in designing a research project with a strong decision focus. Some people will feel naturally hesitant about their first meeting with a client. Most students will have taken only one or two marketing courses. It should not be surprising if many people in your group do not yet *feel* like experts.

Nevertheless, that may be just what your client expects. The client's willingness to cooperate may depend on the perception your team creates during the first meeting. Little need be said about the importance of appropriate attire and behavior. Beyond this, however, your client's perception of your professionalism will be affected strongly by your ability to ask intelligent questions. A good guideline is to focus on a few key areas:

1. Understanding the business

2. Market segmentation

3. Marketing strategy

4. What the manager knows, thinks, or assumes about issues in each of these areas

Throughout this project manual, we will use an example focused on a particular business, Apex Dry Cleaning. Consider the following initial discussion between a group of student consultants and Ms. Allen, the owner of Apex Dry Cleaning.

John: Ms. Allen, our job as student consultants is to gather information about your customers that might help you in developing better marketing strategies. There will be no charge to you for doing this study. The purpose of this meeting is for us to become familiar with your business and to explore how we might be able to contribute. After this meeting, we will prepare a research proposal outlining how we feel we can help you. We will send you a copy of the proposal and then arrange another meeting to discuss our ideas. You will, of course, have final approval of the project.

Ms. Allen: Fine, I've never thought much about doing marketing research in the past. I've assumed it would be far too expensive for a small business like mine. However, your offer sounds too attractive to turn down.

Jane: Perhaps a good way to start would be for you to tell us something about the background of your business.

Ms. Allen: Well, I opened my business in this location about ten years ago. At the time, I had only one employee besides myself. We barely broke even for the first few years. But, as you probably know, this area of the city has grown a great deal, and we have grown with it. By the fifth year of operation, we began to feel really successful. We enjoy a good profit, and I am able to provide a good life-style for myself and my family.

John: Who do you consider to be your main competitors?

Ms. Allen: That is hard to say. The dry cleaning business is very competitive. It is not uncommon to see an establishment open and then close within six months. The large chains are probably the hardest for us to compete with. They have lower average costs and substantial advertising budgets. Comet and One Hour are in small shopping centers just up the street. They both opened just after I opened my store. So I assume that they are successful. Also, there is Arrow Cleaners in the strip shopping center about a mile the other way.

Larry: How do you think your establishment is different from the others you just mentioned?

Ms. Allen: I'd like to think that we offer a higher-quality product than the others. I've spent a great deal of time training my employees and try to compensate them in such a way that they will stay with me. I feel that we put more care into our product than the others do. We would like every piece of dry cleaning to be perfect.

Larry: Do you think that this higher quality is apparent to your customers?

Ms. Allen: I know it is to some. Customers often compliment us on the good job we do. Yesterday, a gentleman told me that he had looked for years for a cleaners that would do his neckties the way he liked. But I'm not sure that all my customers feel the same way. I think some people are very conscious of their clothing and appreciate the fact that we are as concerned with its care as they are. On the other hand, there are probably others to whom one dry cleaner is as good as another. It just doesn't make a lot of difference.

John: That makes me wonder about those people to whom all dry cleaners are alike. Why do you suppose they patronize your store?

Ms. Allen: Oh, it could be simple convenience. We have a pretty nice location and get good exposure to drive-by traffic.

Mary Beth: How about your prices, compared to the competition?

Ms. Allen: We are probably a little more expensive than the chains and about the same as One-Hour. We feel that we take more care than the others, doing things like prespotting, replacing buttons, and making minor repairs. Those things add to our costs, but at least to some customers, it is apparently worth it.

Larry: How do you set your prices?

Ms. Allen: I periodically observe how much time goes into the care of each garment to estimate the costs. Then I base my prices on a multiple of those costs. You know, it puzzles me. I charge $1.35 for men's shirts, but Comet charges 79 cents. I don't know how they do it. That would barely cover my costs.

Jane: How about your target market? Do you think you attract the same types of customers as your competitors?

Ms. Allen: That is a very good question and one I often think about. I think the people who come here are a little more likely to be younger, in their twenties and early thirties, not rich but at least solid white collar. There seem to be quite a few students. It seems that I see more Cadillacs and Mercedes in One-Hour's parking lot than I do in mine. It also seems to me that a relatively large number of my customers are women. I've seen some data in *Dry Cleaning News* about the garment mix of the average dry cleaners. We do more women's dresses and fewer men's suits than the average.

Larry: How do you promote your business? Do you do any advertising?

Ms. Allen: About once a month, I run an ad in both the local newspaper and in the campus newspaper offering coupons for specials on slacks, skirts, shirts, and blouses. They seem to be fairly effective, especially the ones on shirts and blouses. Twice a year, I have flyers distributed. I try to cover an area within a three mile radius of the store.

John: How did you choose those particular coupons?

Ms. Allen: Well, those seem to be the ones that most dry cleaners use. If you are getting at whether they are the right ones for me, I would have to say I'm not sure.

Larry: Do you honor your competitor's coupons?

Ms. Allen: Yes, and you know it's interesting that I don't get many competitor's coupons. Most of the coupon users are our regular customers, and they usually use ours. It kind of concerns me that all I'm doing is giving lower prices to customers I would have gotten anyway. I guess that's why we don't go to a lot of trouble to point out that we honor competitor's coupons.

Mary Beth: Are there any particular marketing ideas that you have been considering as a way of expanding your business?

Ms. Allen: I've often wondered whether a pickup and delivery service might be attractive to some people. More and more families have both spouses working. If people liked it, I'm not sure how much we would charge. I've also thought about different types of coupons, such as one dollar off on a ten dollar order to try to be more price competitive with the chains. And some people have said that they think my sign is too small.

Jane: Well, Ms. Allen, you have certainly given us a lot of information about the dry cleaning business and a lot of food for thought. I'm wondering, can you think of any places where we might go for additional background on the dry cleaning business?

Ms. Allen: I mentioned *Dry Cleaning News,* which is a publication that I and other store owners subscribe to. It has a lot of information about the dry cleaning business. Most of the articles are about cleaning techniques and methods, but occasionally, there are articles about marketing. There are probably even some that I have missed, I'm always so busy. There may also be other publications I don't subscribe to.

John: Do you keep old issues?

Ms. Allen: Yes, I do, for a while. I have a box full of them right behind my desk. Would you like to take them?

Jane: That would be great. *Dry Cleaning News* might be a little hard to find in the campus library. Is there anything else you think we should know that we haven't asked about, some additional information that might be useful to you?

Ms. Allen: I can't think of anything off the top of my head. Your group seems to have asked all the right questions, even about things I haven't given a lot of thought to. Maybe you can tell me how Comet can do shirts for seventy-nine cents.

Looking back on the conversation, a number of questions should occur to you that were not asked. And you should be able to see how a number of answers to the questions could have been explored in greater detail. However, this hypothetical conversation is typical. During the brief discussion, the group encouraged Ms. Allen to talk about the market segment she was serving and market segments in which she might not be doing well. Characteristics of her product mix were explored. Her pricing and the price sensitivity of her customers were discussed. Some attention was given both to present and future locations. A variety of different advertising and promotional methods were also revealed. Finally, the group learned of a source of background information that might provide research ideas and objectives not suggested by the conversation.

A number of the questions asked of Ms. Allen will be found to be useful in most marketing research studies. Others are of indirect relevance. For instance, if the client were the student counseling and testing service (offered free of charge), it would appear that questions about price would not apply. However, thinking more broadly, we might see how there is an issue of price with regard to convenience and the psychological cost of seeking help with study habits or career choices. Likewise, the product attributes of counseling and testing might be less obvious. The benefit sought might be "more confidence in career choices," as opposed to well-maintained clothing.

You should also note not only what was said in the conversation but how it was said. In nearly all of Ms. Allen's responses, we find such phrases as "that is hard to say," "I assume," "I think," and "it seems." This is not to imply that Ms. Allen is not knowledgeable about her business. She has obviously formed a number of impressions based upon frequent observation and contact with her customers. However, she would probably admit that there is very little about which she is certain. And it is likely that she would not feel totally comfortable making major strategic decisions with the information that she presently has.

Ms. Allen's uncertainty about her customers and competitive environment offers an excellent opportunity for the group to provide her with valuable information. Even if nothing new, unique, or surprising is revealed by the research study, the findings should serve to reduce her uncertainty and provide her with a basis for stronger confidence in what she believes. It is also possible that a few of her beliefs will be discovered to be without foundation, providing a basis for caution and encouragement for further exploration.

Appendix 3A contains a client interview form that you could use to guide you in asking key questions during the client interview. It is unlikely to include all of the important questions you will want to ask the client. However it should encourage you to explore the major areas of marketing strategy.

APPENDIX 3A
CLIENT INTERVIEW FORM

NAME OF FIRM _____

ADDRESS_____

CONTACT _____ PHONE _____

GENERAL INFORMATION:

Years in operation and background:_____

_____

_____

Major products, product lines, or services:_____

_____

_____

CUSTOMERS:

Geographical distribution:_____

Descriptive Characteristics (Age, Sex, Income, Occupation, Marital Status etc.):_____

_____

_____

_____

Do you have customer groups that differ significantly from each other? If so, How? _____

_____

_____

Are there groups of customers you think you should be reaching but aren't? If so, what do you think is the reason they aren't being reached?

_____

_____

Are all of your potential customer groups sufficiently aware of your product or service. If yes, why do you think that? If not, why not?

_____

_____

COMPETITION:

Who do you believe to be your major competitors and what is (are) the particular strength (s) of each?

COMPETITOR	MAJOR STRENGTHS
_____	_____
_____	_____
_____	_____
_____	_____
_____	_____

PRICING:

How important is pricing in maintaining your competitive position? _____

_____

How are your prices compared to your competitors? _____

_____

How do you set your prices or make price changes? _____

_____

ADVERTISING:

How important is advertising in maintaining your competitive position? _____

_____

What does your advertising say?_____

_____

How much (or how often) do you advertise? _____

_____

Where do you advertise? _____

_____

Do your competitors advertise more or less than you do? _____

_____

Do you think their advertising is effective? _____

_____

SALES PROMOTION:

Are sales, special prices, coupons, or other promotional items important to the success of your business?

_____

_____

Which kinds do you and your competitors use? _____

_____

_____

Do you use these methods to attract new customers or to build loyalty among existing customers?

_____

DISTRIBUTION OR LOCATION:

How important is distribution or location in maintaining your competitive position?

_____

How is your location compared to your competitors? _____

_____

PERSONAL SELLING AND CUSTOMER SERVICE:

How important is personal selling and/or customer service in maintaining your competitive position?

_____

How is your sales staff compared to your competitors? _____

_____

MAJOR DECISIONS:

Are there major decisions in any area of your business that you are contemplating within the next year?

Decision # 1: _____

Major alternatives: _____

Greatest uncertainty about alternatives: _____

What would you like to know that would help reduce this uncertainty? _____

_____

Decision # 2: _____

Major alternatives: _____

Greatest uncertainty about alternatives: _____

What would you like to know that would help reduce this uncertainty? _____

_____

OTHER INFORMATION:

CHAPTER FOUR
THE RESEARCH PROPOSAL

PURPOSE OF THE RESEARCH PROPOSAL

A full description of your marketing research project will be contained in the research proposal. The proposal is a very important document because it performs a number of functions:

1. It contains an outline of the steps of the project and will serve as a valuable reference.

2. It reflects your thinking about the topic and the decisions you have made about the most appropriate research methods.

3. It provides a checkpoint for comparing your goals and objectives with those of the client.

4. Once agreed to, it represents a "contract" between you and the client regarding the work to be performed.

In Chapter One, we described an outline of the marketing research process. The proposal will reflect your thinking about the first several steps of this process and your judgment about how to perform the subsequent steps. Proposals vary dramatically in length. When the client and the researcher have a complete verbal understanding of the project, the proposal may be as short as a page or two, providing little more than a brief description of the project and a time and cost estimate. On the other hand, a proposal may be over a hundred of pages in length (e.g., proposals to perform work for governmental organizations), fully describing the background and qualifications of the research company and providing great detail about the design of the project. The length of the proposal usually depends upon its purpose. If the client is confident in the researcher and is not choosing among bidders, a document that briefly describes what is to be done may be sufficient. On the other hand, in a bidding situation, the client may use the document as a primary tool in the evaluation of suppliers. In this case, it should include a complete discussion that supports the design decisions that have been made (or in your case, allows the instructor to evaluate the quality of your reasoning).

Table 4.1 contains an outline of a typical research proposal:

TABLE 4.1
OUTLINE OF THE RESEARCH PROPOSAL

I.   Background Investigation
II.   Research Objectives
III.   Research Methodology
    A.   Data Gathering Method
    B.   Sampling Plan
    C.   Discussion of Data Gathering Instrument
    D.   Data Collection
IV.   Tabulation and Data Analysis
V.   Research Reporting
VI.   Time and Cost Estimates
VII. Limitations

BACKGROUND INVESTIGATION

Client Interview. An important step in the research process involves a thorough background investigation. Many professional researchers admit that this step is often overlooked. A fundamental part of this investigation is your meeting with the client. In Chapter Three, we described a conversation of a research team with their client. In the proposal, you should devote a couple of paragraphs to a summary of your interpretations of this conversation.

Occasionally, the researchers will discover that previous studies have been done for the client. These studies should be carefully reviewed. They may provide useful information that the researchers can use, such as questionnaires and research results. (Note: If the client provides you with old questionnaires, you should make this fact known to your instructor. He or she may not object to your referring to them but may want to ensure that your work is original and, perhaps, represents some improvement on the original research methodology).

Trade Publications. Another source of valuable background material is trade publications. Recall that the study group requested copies of *Dry Cleaning News*, a magazine read by dry cleaning proprietors. You may find that the collection of trade publications at your university library is not as good as that found in the main public library of a large city, since these publications are of more general interest to the public at large. Several issues, perhaps those from the preceding year, should be reviewed to try to find information of use to the person responsible for the research design. Such a review might uncover articles regarding:

1. Current and innovative marketing practices in the industry. These often provide alternative marketing methods to be evaluated.

2. Successful marketing strategies. These can generate ideas for future marketing plans.

3. Industry trends and statistics on growth rate, sales, and profitability. These can serve as useful standards of comparison with the client's business.

4. The results of previous surveys of firms within the industry. It is very common for trade associations, who often sponsor the trade publication, to conduct industry studies that will provide general information of interest to its members and subscribers. These studies frequently gather data which individual businesses would be reluctant to share directly with their competitors. Past results of these studies can be very useful in suggesting possible questions and question wording, or by providing a basis for comparison of the results of your study with the industry in general.

Having thoroughly reviewed the materials described above, you should prepare a summary of your findings in paragraph form.

RESEARCH OBJECTIVES

Focus on Decisions. The most important part of your research proposal is your listing of objectives, the things you hope to accomplish with your study. Your objectives should focus on information that will help the client make better marketing decisions. Objectives should be as specific as you can make them. A useful starting point is to try to make a list of the potential decisions that have been suggested by the background investigation. Based upon the conversation with Ms. Allen in Chapter Three, we see that she may be contemplating decisions in the areas of:

1. Methods of setting prices.

2. Various types of coupons that might evoke desirable consumer responses.

3. A possible new location.

4.   Consideration of a delivery service.

5.   A new sign.

Other Potential Decisions. In addition to the obvious impending decisions mentioned by the client, a number of longer-range decisions may be implied by the initial conversation. We note that Ms. Allen expressed some degree of uncertainty in a number of areas. For instance, she believes that her customers are willing to pay a price premium for a higher-quality product. This opinion may reflect her biases and may not be widely shared by all customers. If this is the case, one alternative would be a general price reduction to attract more price-sensitive customers. Another would be a price reduction directed to specific groups through the use of a money-off coupon. This suggests an additional managerial decision in that these price-sensitive customers must be identified in order to direct the offer primarily to them. Some other areas of uncertainty that were raised in the discussion with Ms Allen include:

1.   The definition of the target market.

2.   Consumer perceptions of quality.

3.   The trade-off between price and quality.

4.   The motivations of competitors in setting prices in an "irrational" manner.

A Model of Consumer Response. The *Hierarchy of Effects* model suggests an interesting approach to thinking about information to be obtained from customers. This model states that a person moves through a series of psychological stages of commitment regarding things he or she experiences (persons, ideas, products, etc.). For example, consider the development of your friendship with another person. This would begin with your first becoming aware of the person and then learning things about him or her. Finding that you share many common interests, you might find you like the person and even that you prefer his or her company to the company of others. Later, a level of commitment and loyalty to the friend may develop. Note that each stage in this commitment process depends upon the previous stage. This same model could be applied to most of the things that become a part of our lives. Clearly, with most things, we do not get beyond simple awareness. However, with others, higher levels of commitment are achieved. One version of a hierarchical model has six stages and can be applied to a product or service as follows:

Awareness. Before a person can respond to a brand he or she must first become aware of its existence.

Knowledge. Having achieved some level of awareness, the person next acquires knowledge of the brand that allows it to be differentiated from other brands.

Liking. Of those brands the consumer can evaluate, some are considered acceptable candidates for a purchase while others are not.

Preference. Of those brands that are considered acceptable, some are preferred over others.

Commitment. Preference leads to some level of commitment as evidenced by a purchase or intention to purchase.

Conviction. The development of a strong preference for a brand may lead to conviction as evidenced by brand loyalty.

The above model is referred to as hierarchical because each successive stage depends upon previous stages. Many scholars agree that it applies to a wide variety of consumer purchase situations. Managers are interested in the hierarchy because each stage represents a different level of consumer response to marketing actions. Products are designed with regard to consumer likes and preferences. Price is also used to influence liking or preference. Advertising initially influences consumer awareness and knowledge. Additional advertising, along with other promotional items such as coupons, influences preferences, purchase intentions and helps to build brand loyalty. Thus, measurements that identify the consumer's present stage in the hierarchy enable managers to evaluate the effectiveness of their marketing strategies. For example, there could be a number explanations for low brand sales. If it is determined that brand awareness is extremely low, additional advertising or more careful specification of media would be called for. On the other hand, if awareness is high but very few consumers have tried the product, it is possible that the benefits provided by the product do not appeal to them. A high level of trial but a low level of repeat purchasing could indicate that the product is not delivering the benefits that consumers expect from the product.

Descriptive Characteristics. Most segmentation and/or positioning studies will also include customer descriptive characteristics (referred to as demographic, psychographic and socioeconomic status). These could include such items as age, sex, income, family composition, marital status, and education. The research designer should select descriptive characteristics that are expected to be related to customer response to the marketing strategy. For instance, family size might be closely related to the level of peanut butter purchasing. On the other hand, it may be of little value to know a person's religious affiliation if the study is intended to investigate people's motivations for choosing a particular peanut butter brand.

Other Information. Another area that is sometimes included in the objectives is consumer media habits. Media habits can be identified simply and straightforwardly, with questions such as "Which daily newspaper do you read," or more extensively, with questions such as "On which days are you most likely to read the newspaper," or "What sections do you read on a regular basis?"

Describing Objectives. Below are some common objectives of segmentation and/or positioning studies that might be suggested by the hierarchy of effects model.

1. To measure consumer awareness of brands in the product/service category.

2. To determine if consumers know the differentiating characteristics of brands in the category (e.g., Heinz is the catsup that pours slower).

3. To determine consumer awareness of advertising and recall of copy.

4. To measure consumer perceptions of important brand attributes in the areas of product, price, and distribution.

5. To measure the importance that consumers place on various brand attributes in making choices in the product category.

6. To determine present and potential media as sources for information about the brand.

7. To measure relevant descriptive characteristics of groups defined by the above attitudinal and behavior aspects (e.g., those aware of the brand versus those who are not, buyers versus nonbuyers)

Many managerial decision objectives would be supported by measures focusing on the stages in the hierarchy. Usually, when there are specific decision alternatives to be evaluated, a greater amount of detail may be provided in a particular area of the *Hierarchy of Effects*. For instance, some additional objectives for Apex Dry Cleaning might be:

1. To evaluate the relative desirability of various types of coupon offers.

2. To determine the target market most likely to be influenced by these offers.

3. To determine the most efficient ways of getting these coupons into the hands of the members of selected target markets.

RESEARCH METHODOLOGY

The next section of the research proposal discusses the methodology the project group will use to conduct the study. It will reflect a number of important decisions that the group has made. Typically, such decisions are made sequentially by evaluating the relative desirability of each of several research approaches. Below is a brief outline of some important methodological decisions:

> **Secondary Data**
> **Primary Data**
> > **Observation**
> > **Experimentation**
> > **Survey**
> > > **Telephone**
> > > **Personal or Intercept Interview**
> > > **Self-Administered Questionnaire**

Each decision is discussed below.

Secondary or Primary Data. The first decision that would normally be made is whether to utilize only secondary data, only primary data or a combination of both. Actually, the use of secondary data alone is not an option for your group since the project requires the conduct of a survey. However, it will add an air of completeness to your proposal if you discuss why primary data are to be preferred in accomplishing your research objectives.

Secondary data are data that may be obtained from existing sources. Census data, published surveys, data from syndicated resources, and the internal records of the company are examples. Secondary data are often overlooked by marketing researchers, although when used creatively, they can solve a wide variety of marketing problems without resort to primary sources. For example, suppose a company that markets heavy equipment to manufacturing firms wants to estimate the sales potential in a new geographical territory. One approach would be to survey potential customers in the new area to obtain information about their current and intended purchasing behavior. However, an alternative approach might rely on internal company data about sales to customers in existing territories. This data could then be extrapolated to the new market area through the use of census data (e.g., *The Census of Manufacturing of the United States*). Thus, secondary data can often be used to solve marketing problems quickly and economically without resort to more expensive and time-consuming primary data.

Typically, secondary data will not provide all of the decision-making information needed by the client. In this case, the researcher must turn to primary data, those that are gathered specifically to solve the problem at hand. For instance, it would be impossible to find secondary information about consumer attitudes towards *Apex Dry Cleaners*.   In this situation, primary data will have to be gathered directly from consumers in a custom-designed marketing research project.

Observation, Experimentation or Survey. Having chosen primary data, the next important decision involves the type of data to be employed. As with primary or secondary data, this does not represent a decision that your research group will need to make. However, for the sake of completeness, you could discuss why a survey is particularly appropriate for accomplishing your research objectives. Three major categories of primary data are observational studies, experimentation, and surveys.

Observation is a desirable research technique when the researcher wants to measure customer behavior without intervention. Counting traffic to determine the number of prospective customers passing through an intersection is a typical example of observation. Traffic counts are often a key component of site location studies. The observational method can provide highly unbiased information about how customers behave. However, it would not be useful in telling us what the consumer knows, feels, or intends to do in the future.

Experimentation is another primary research technique that is used when the purpose of the study is to perform a careful evaluation of a small number of marketing alternatives. This type of research is designed to explore cause-and-effect relationships. Experiments may be performed in the laboratory, as when taste testing product flavors, or in the field. Some types of field experiments provide a natural setting for testing consumer responses to price changes, package redesign, shelf placement, and store displays. In-home usage testing allows consumers and their families to experience new products in the ways that they use the products in their every day lives. Experimentation often follows, and is influenced by, the results of surveys. For instance, a survey may be used to reduce a large number of alternatives to a smaller number that may be more carefully evaluated through experimentation.

On the other hand, when the researcher is interested in "state of mind" measures, it is necessary to directly question the consumer through the use of a survey. An observational study cannot be used to measure consumer brand awareness and experimentation, which may become desirable once the research problem is carefully defined, may be premature at this point. For the accomplishment of the objectives discussed earlier, a survey is required. Your textbook discusses additional considerations in the choice of the survey versus experimentation or observation

What Type of Survey? If a survey is necessary to accomplish your client's objectives, the next important decision is the type of survey to be performed. Three important forms are telephone interviewing, personal interviewing through intercept methods, and the self-administered questionnaire (either mailed or sometimes handed to the respondent in an intercept fashion). Any of these approaches may be appropriate for your marketing research project. Your choice will depend upon the suitability of each method in accomplishing your objectives.

The advantages and disadvantages of each method are extensively discussed in your textbook. You will find that no single method will be the best on each important criterion. The choice of a methodology is almost always a trade-off of the advantages and disadvantages of each method. At this point in your proposal, you should explain why you have chosen a particular approach and why other methods were rejected. Other than the objectives, the choice of a survey research technique is probably your most important research issue. It strongly influences subsequent decisions, such as sampling, questionnaire design, and data collection.

SAMPLING PLAN

Purpose of Sampling. The ultimate goal of a survey is to provide representative information about a group from which the sample was drawn. In this part of your proposal, you will define the target population and outline the procedures you are going to use to choose this sample. As with the objectives and methodology, the development of a sampling plan represents a set of decisions made by the research designer. Often, many decisions about sample design must be made simultaneously. For instance, if the research designers want the opinions of college students in general, consideration must be given not only to specifying the population but also how a sampling of such students would be obtained. Chapter Six of this manual and your text discuss a number of issues related to the development of samples.

Your sample size and sampling methods may not be the same as those used in a commercial marketing research study. This is due to time and cost factors. Your sample size will probably be determined by your instructor, who may require each member of the group to conduct a certain number of interviews. Collecting data will be a real learning experience. However, little would be gained by your investing a great amount of time into gathering data. Therefore, your instructor may also allow you considerable latitude in choosing a sampling method since the "best" sampling methods can be extremely expensive in terms of time and resources. Thus, your small sample size and the method you choose may create some inherent limitations to the ultimate usefulness of your results.

Target Population. The first sampling issue involves your definition of the target population. You will use the results of your survey to generalize about attitudes, beliefs, and behaviors of this population. This is very important to keep in mind when defining the population. Looking at the question from the other direction, we might ask, "Once the results of the survey are in, who will we be able to say something about?" For instance, a common mistake students make is to measure the image of their own university by surveying the student body. This is not appropriate if the purpose of the study is to explore ways to enhance the image of the university among prospective students or the community in general.

Populations may be defined with varying degrees of specificity. Examples of definitions of a student population would include:

> All students.
> All undergraduate students.
> All full time undergraduate students.
> All full time day undergraduate students who are not a member of a professional organization.
> All full time day students who live in campus housing.

Note that these population definitions vary in their specificity and each would require somewhat different procedures in developing a sample.

Sampling Method. Having decided on the group of interest, you will then choose a method of gathering a sample from that population. Chapter Six of this manual will discuss a number of sampling methods and describes in detail procedures for obtaining some common types of samples. After considering the various ways of conducting a sample, you should discuss the pros and cons of various methods that may be used in your study and explain why you have chosen a particular method. Next, you should carefully describe the procedures you will use in selecting the members of the sample.

Sampling Accuracy. A final sampling issue to consider is sampling accuracy. Your text discusses procedures for determining sample sizes that will produce a desired level of accuracy. Typically, however, instructors will require students to each conduct between twenty and thirty interviews. In a group of six students, this will result in a sample size of only 120 to 180. Thus, for your purposes, we are concerned with the sampling accuracy produced by a given sample size. This will be discussed more fully in Chapters Six and Eight. For now, you can use Table 4.2 as a guide The table tells you that if your sample size were 100 and if 50 percent of the sample replied "Yes" on a yes/no question, the true value in the population is between 40.2 percent and 59.8 percent (fifty percent plus or minus 9.8 percent) with a 95% level of confidence.

DATA GATHERING INSTRUMENT

It will not be necessary to say a great deal about your questionnaire in the research proposal. Questionnaire design is the next step after the proposal is approved. In fact, you have already implied a great deal about your questionnaire in stating the objectives of the study. However, it is desirable to outline the broad areas of information (awareness, attitudes, descriptive characteristics, etc.) that will be addressed. It is also appropriate to summarize the procedures you will use for pretesting, revising, and obtaining client approval of the data-gathering instrument. Your marketing research text discusses the value of careful pretesting.

TABLE 4.2
Sampling Accuracy on a Yes/No Question
for Various Sample Sizes
(95 % Level of Confidence)

Sample Size	Sampling Accuracy(+ or -)
50	13.9%
75	11.3%
100	9.8%
120	8.9%
140	8.3%
160	7.7%
180	7.3%
200	6.9%
250	6.2%
300	5.7%
500	4.4%

DATA COLLECTION

This section of the proposal should discuss the time frame within which data gathering will take place and the responsibilities of each group member. It should also include procedures and responsibilities for tracking the progress of the work. Finally, procedures for screening questionnaires for accuracy and completeness as well as coding procedures for open-ended questions should be discussed.

DATA ENTRY, TABULATION AND ANALYSIS

This section will discuss how the data contained in the pencil and paper instrument will be transcribed into a machine-readable form. The methods you will use to code open-ended questions should be discussed. The procedures for data entry should also be described. This section also includes a brief discussion of the type of computer resources required, the computer program to be used for tabulation, and the expected tabulation procedures that will be used. (e.g., frequency distributions, cross-tabulations and summary statistical measures etc). If sophisticated analysis methods are to be employed (e.g., regression analysis or perceptual mapping) the rationale for using them should be presented along with a discussion of how they will serve to accomplish the research objectives.

RESEARCH REPORT

In this section, briefly describe what will be included in the final report, noting the types of analysis to be performed and stating that conclusions will be drawn from the data and recommendations will be made. If an oral presentation is to be made, you should mention it in this section and describe how it will differ from the written presentation. A comment on the disposition of the survey material should also be made. Sometimes, students turn the questionnaires over to the instructor or, perhaps, to the client. Often, however, respondents are promised anonymity in return for their participation in the study. If their identity is provided on the questionnaire (for purposes of follow-up or some other reason), then the client should not be given access to them.

TIME AND COST ESTIMATES

In this section of the proposal, you should establish time lines for completing the various phases of the project. An interesting way to do this is with a PERT diagram (see your marketing research textbook for a discussion of using PERT in project scheduling). A PERT diagram lists all of the important project steps in their proper sequences, noting those that must be done sequentially and those that may be done simultaneously. Next, time estimates (usually in terms of person-hours) are attached to each activity. This allows tracing through the various paths of the diagram to identify the maximum amount of time that the project should take (referred to as the critical path). Slack time is also identified for those activities off the critical path that may be delayed without delaying the overall project.

If you choose to not use a PERT diagram, you should at least present a table that lists the various important tasks to be performed (e.g. questionnaire designed, data gathered, etc.) and specify a date for the completion of each. This should help you to appreciate how vitally important it is that the various activities be completed in on time. Appendix 4A provides an outline of the survey research process including most of the essential activities you will complete. Items that your instructor may ask you to turn in for review are especially critical.

Although your project is to be done at little or no cost to the client, your instructor may want you to estimate what the project would cost if the value of the students time were, for example, one hundred dollars per hour for professional work and fifteen dollars per hour for actual interviewing. This can be done from the PERT diagram by simply adding up the total person-hours required for the activities and applying a billing rate that you feel would be appropriate for similar professional services.

LIMITATIONS

The limitations section of the proposal (and final report) is very important. Any marketing research study will have at least some limitation and this is especially true in the case of student projects. As mentioned earlier, the design of any research project involves many decisions and each decision usually involves a trade off of a number of advantages and disadvantages. A number of limitations of the study should occur to you. These would include limits on:

1.   the ability of the students to conduct a professional marketing research study.

2.   the statistical precision of the results due to the small sample size.

3.   the ability to generalize the results due to the specification of the population.

4.   the ability to obtain a good sample frame with which to represent the population.

5.   the number of areas to be explored due to the shortness of the questionnaire.

6.   potential biases such as noncontact, refusals, and respondent non-cooperation.

Once your research proposal is prepared, you will turn it in to your instructor. Appendix 4B provides a checklist you may want to use to ensure that you have addressed all of the important elements of the research proposal. To save time, you should also give a copy to the client. Alternatively, you might wait until the instructor has returned the proposal so that you can incorporate his or her suggestions and recommendations before giving the final version of the proposal to the client.

CONCLUSION

It should be clear that the research proposal is a very important document and, once it is completed, it provides a guide for the conduct of the remainder of your study. Once the proposal is approved, any deviations from the proposed methodology should be agreed to by your instructor and by your client.

An additional benefit of a good research proposal will be its usefulness in writing the research report. First, for the purpose of completeness, the research report should describe the research methodology. If you adhere closely to the proposal, the initial sections of the final report will require only a minor rewrite of the proposal. Second, in discussing your research results, the proposal, especially its objectives, will provide an invaluable guide in constructing a useful document.

APPENDIX 4A
ESTIMATED TIMELINE OF PROJECT ACTIVITIES

TEAM # _____   Client_____

Project Title_____

ACTIVITY	EXPECTED COMPLETION DATE
Project Ideas Submitted*	_____
Project Idea Approved	_____
Meeting With Client	_____
Proposal Submitted*	_____
Proposal Approved	_____
Rough Draft of Questionnaire Submitted*	_____
Sampling Plan	_____
Questionnaire Pretest	_____
Questionnaire Revised and Printed	_____
Data Gathering Completed	_____
Coding	_____
Analysis Program Prepared	_____
Data Entry	_____
Preliminary Tabulations	_____
Preliminary Analysis	_____
Final Analysis and Report*	_____

*Items to be turned in to instructor for review.

Additional Notes:

APPENDIX 4B
RESEARCH PROPOSAL CHECKLIST

TEAM # _____   **Client** _____

Project Title _____

PROPOSAL SECTION	COMPLETED
Summary Description of Project	_____
Background Investigation:	
Summary of Client Interview	_____
Other Background Information	_____
Research Objectives	_____
Research Methodology:	
Data Gathering Method	_____
Sampling Plan and Sample Size	_____
Data Gathering Instrument	_____
Pretest	_____
Data Collection Procedures	_____
Coding, Tabulation, and Analysis Procedures	_____
Research Report	_____
Time and Cost Estimates	_____
Limitations	_____

Additional Notes:

CHAPTER FIVE
QUESTIONNAIRE DESIGN

The goal of questionnaire design is to translate the research objectives into questions that will elicit the desired information. The design of a questionnaire may, at first, appear simple. In fact, it is often quite difficult. Your text discusses a number of general issues related to measurement, questionnaire construction, and attitude scaling. In this chapter, we will focus on the task of developing a questionnaire for a study such as yours. Appendix 5A provides a brief sample questionnaire for the Apex Dry Cleaners study. With a few exceptions, we will use questions from this sample questionnaire to illustrate the information provided in Chapter 5. In later chapters, we will use the same sample questionnaire as the basis for illustrating data analysis and the research report.

FROM OBJECTIVES TO QUESTIONS

What Information Is Needed? The accomplishment of the research objectives requires carefully specifying the information to be acquired. For instance, consider the objective of "measuring consumer awareness of brands in a product category." It is the researcher's job to decide on appropriate measures of awareness. For instance, what do we mean by awareness? Is it recall without prompting? Could recall be measured by asking if the respondent has heard of various brands when the interviewer reads from a list? Will we require the respondent to recall something about the brand in addition to its name? Another issue is to determine which brands are to be measured. Are we only interested in the client's brand? Near competitors? Indirect competitors?

Translating Information Needs into Questions. Even though the researcher has a clear concept of the desired information, communication between the interviewer and the subject may present a number of hurdles to be overcome. Consider the deceptively simple question:

What is your annual income?

This question could have many possible meanings to the respondent. To some, "your income" could mean family income. Some will think of income from their primary job, others may include income from such sources as investments. One subject may think of income before taxes, while others will think of take-home pay. What is the "income" of a college student who depends on his or her parents for living expenses and has a part-time job? Considering all of the possible interpretations of the income question, a preferred form might be illustrated by the following question which is similar to Question 16 from Appendix 5A:

Please tell me the total income of the household in which you live from all sources before taxes in the last calendar year. Include support you received from relatives, scholarships, grants, or any other source.

GENERAL QUESTIONNAIRE DESIGN GUIDELINES

It is the research designer's job to facilitate a smooth, flowing conversation between the interviewer and the person providing the information. The research designer must constantly view the interviewing process from the perspective of the interviewee. Respondents are sure to have different educational backgrounds, experiences and life styles. Communication between any two people depends upon a common perspective. While designing the questionnaire, researchers must often play the role of their own subjects.

Will the Respondent Understand the Question? The questionnaire must communicate as clearly and accurately as possible. Two major sources of error in marketing research studies are (a) different people understanding the question differently and (b) the respondent not fully understanding the question but answering it anyway. You should try to break long, complex sentences into short ones and use words that the respondent will understand without misinterpretation. Consider the inherent difficulties in the following questions:

How often do you eat Sunday dinner at home?

What is your favorite entree?

What is the meaning of "dinner"? Do all subjects have the same concept of what is meant by an "entree"?

In writing your questionnaire, you and your research group should scrutinize each word of each question, asking yourselves if it could be interpreted in different ways by different people. If different interpretations are possible, you should consider rewording the question. Otherwise, you may not be measuring the same thing from each subject.

Does the Respondent Know the Answer? A second important consideration is whether the respondent has the ability to answer. Note the difficulty of the following question:

> **How much do you owe on your current automobile loan?**

While most people probably know the value of their monthly payment on their auto loan, few could accurately estimate the loan balance without consulting their records.

It is not uncommon to find questionnaires in which researchers ask questions about which respondents have no knowledge at all, such as:

> **How much Social Security tax did you pay last year?**

This question should probably be eliminated or revised.

Can the Respondent Recall the Answer? Another important consideration is that the respondent must recall the information. It may be difficult for an interviewee to answer a question such as:

> **How much money did you spend in restaurants in the past year?**

The respondent surely knew the amount of the bill when each check was paid. However, the answer to this question requires a cumulation of data from many purchases over a long period of time. The information is not easily recalled. Besides the difficulty of remembering the amount spent, the question is confusing. It is not clear whether we are asking about the respondent's own meals or any meals purchased. Are fast-food establishments considered restaurants? Are university dining facilities included? A question that would be more likely to generate an accurate response would be:

> **In the past week, how much money did you spend in any type of eating establishment on meals for yourself?**

If the researcher is interested in annual spending, it could be calculated from the more accurate weekly data.

The Respondent Must Be Willing to Provide the Information. Sometimes marketing researchers must deal with sensitive topics. Questions about products used in the bathroom or about moral issues may be very difficult to ask. Would you feel comfortable designing (or administering) a questionnaire to measure student awareness and attitudes toward AIDS and the use of condoms? In fact, such studies are routinely performed by professional research organizations. The tendency of respondents to overstate or understate the values being measured is referred to as response bias, and sensitive questions are especially susceptible to this type of error.

Other types of questions that may contain response bias are those dealing with normative data. Normative data is information that the respondent feels might allow the interviewer to form a positive or negative impression. Information about income or education may be subject to this type of bias. Other people may be sensitive about revealing their age. Numerous studies have shown that people are likely to overestimate the frequency with which they engage in socially desirable behaviors; watching public television is an example. Later, we will provide an example of how to ask such questions so as to minimize the bias that might be caused by normative content.

QUESTION FORM

The two major question forms are open-ended and closed-ended. While many questions may be asked in either form, each has advantages and disadvantages for eliciting different types of information. Your text discusses this issue in detail. We will briefly summarize some of the considerations that are relevant to your study.

Open-Ended Questions. Open-ended questions provide the respondent with a specific question but allow considerable latitude in answering. Open-ended questions are usually used when the researcher does not want to prompt the respondent with possible answers or when the breadth of possible answers is difficult to anticipate.

Open-ended questions are widely used in depth interviewing, a research technique sometimes employed to generate insights and ideas in order to familiarize the researcher with a problem prior to designing more structured research studies. Depth interviews may be composed almost entirely of open-ended questions. However, they are usually performed by extremely well-trained and well-briefed interviewers who are experienced in using this technique. The goal of depth interviews is to encourage the respondent to provide more than superficial answers. Interviewers continue to dig deeper with follow-up questions, such as "Why do you feel that way?" or "What do you mean by...?"

Occasionally, segmentation/positioning studies may use open-ended questions in the same manner as depth interviews. More typically, however, open-ended questions are used to generate natural, unaided recall of brand names, advertisements, the content of advertisements, packages, or other marketing stimuli. A typical question to measure unaided brand recall is illustrated by Question 2 of Appendix 5A:

When you think of dry cleaning establishments, which ones come to mind?

The interviewer will record all establishments mentioned, perhaps by checking them off on a list. This type of open-ended question differs from those used in the depth interview. In the brand recall question, we are asking the question in an open-ended fashion but using a closed-ended format to record the responses. Sometimes, for brands not mentioned, the above question would be followed by additional questions to measure aided recall of specific brands or services, such as:

Have you also heard of Apex Dry Cleaners?

Have you also heard of Comet Dry Cleaners?

Another situation in which unaided recall may be used would be to measure advertising impact or awareness. Questions 3 and 4 of Appendix 5A illustrate an open-ended question sequence to measure unaided recall of advertising:

3. **What dry cleaners have you seen any advertisements for in the past month?**

4. **What can you remember that the ads said or showed? (PROBE AND RECORD FIRST TWO THINGS MENTIONED)**

The second question (what the ads said or showed) is a typical open-ended question used when the research designer does not want to bias the natural reaction of the respondent by mentioning the actual advertising copy. The interviewer is directed to probe to get a meaningful response to the question. Careful training and briefing of interviewers is very important to allow them to distinguish between those responses that are meaningful to the objectives of the study and those that are not.

CLOSED-ENDED QUESTIONS

Closed-Ended Questions Require Careful Research Design. When the researcher has done a thorough job of background research and questionnaire design, the questionnaire will often contain mostly closed-ended questions. This type of question presents the respondent with a fixed set of alternative answers. When there are only two possible answers, the response format is called dichotomous. When there are more than two responses, it called multichotomous. Usually the list of possible responses is contained within the questionnaire, although it is common to find a response such as OTHER, SPECIFY _____
which may be used to record unanticipated answers. The SPECIFY portion allows the interviewer to record answers that were not provided on the questionnaire.

The use of closed-ended questions is one of the most important ways that a descriptive study such as yours will differ from an exploratory study, such as a focus group or in-depth interview. In exploratory work, the researcher has only a vague idea of what will be learned. Exploratory studies should help the research designer identify appropriate questions and anticipate many of the possible responses. Their major weaknesses are that the sample sizes are small and unrepresentative and, further, that the responses are difficult to compare across respondents. On the other hand, a descriptive study should be treated as confirmatory. The results of the descriptive study should provide evidence whether or not things discovered in the exploratory phase are truly representative of the population under study.

Closed-Ended Questions Provide the Respondent with Choices. The use of closed-ended questions provides some evidence that the researcher has not only given serious thought to the questions of interest but also has anticipated the possible answers. Consider the following form of a question:

What types of coupons do you prefer to use for dry cleaning?

_____

versus an alternate form taken from Appendix 5A

7.   **When you use coupons, what one type do you most prefer. Would it be (READ LIST BELOW)?**

(19)

Price discounts, such as $ 1 off on a $ 10 order 1
Special prices on suits 2
Special prices on slacks 3
Special prices on laundered shirts and blouses 4
REFUSED OR DON'T KNOW 8

The first question requests that the respondent not only evaluate alternative coupon strategies but also generate the alternative choices. This places a burden on respondents who, in their behavior as consumers, are accustomed to being presented with choice situations, not with creating them. The second form of the question provides the respondent with choices. The job of designing interesting and attractive choices belongs to the marketing manager. This task may be aided by marketing research techniques, such as focus groups and depth interviews, as well as the variety of sources from which new product ideas are generated. However, if an important objective of the study is to _predict_ those alternatives that consumers will find most attractive, it is important that they be presented with all the relevant choices. Suppose that, in response to the first form of the question, a consumer did not mention a certain type of coupon. Does this indicate that the respondent does not prefer it or simply that it was not recalled?

Closed-Ended Questions Provide a Frame of Reference. Unfortunately, the problem of anticipating possible responses causes some researchers to overuse open-ended questions. Consider the following question taken from a student survey conducted at a major theme park:

How did you enjoy your visit to the park today?

The first three completed questionnaires included the following responses:

"It was pretty good."

"We would have had a great time if the kids hadn't been so tired."

"It wasn't as good as yesterday."

A well-trained interviewer, properly briefed to probe for a complete and meaningful response, might have generated additional useful information. However, the above three responses, as well as a majority of those on the remaining questionnaires, were virtually unusable. It is difficult to interpret the meaning of the phrase "pretty good." The second and third responses present the difficulty that the respondents have provided an evaluation by comparison with another experience that is not common across all respondents. Unfortunately for the research group, this question was intended to accomplish one of the major goals of the project; to measure customer satisfaction. A more desirable form of asking this question would have been:

How did you enjoy your visit to the park today? Would you say it was: (INTERVIEWER READ RESPONSES)

     Outstanding
     Excellent
     Good
     Fair
     Poor

Closed-Ended Questions Allow for Easier Coding and Data Analysis. One major disadvantage of open-ended responses is that they must ultimately be placed into closed-ended categories. This means that each open-ended response must be assigned an identifying code so that the data can be entered into the computer for analysis. When the variety of responses is great (as implied by the previous example), this can be difficult and time-consuming. Chapter Seven (and your text) discusses some of the issues involved in coding.

ATTITUDE SCALING

In a typical product/service positioning study, consumer attitudes are measured through the use of scales. Your text discusses a wide variety of procedures for measuring attitudes. However, in a segmentation/positioning study, the most common type is the semantic differential scale. On semantic differential scales, the subject is requested to respond to a set of bipolar adjectives that provide an evaluation of various product attributes or characteristics. The ends of the scale and sometimes points in between may be anchored with words or phrases that indicate a degree of positive or negative feeling toward some characteristic of the object of interest.

In using the semantic differential scale, two important decisions must be made. The first decision relates to the characteristics to be measured. Generating a list of product or service characteristics should not be difficult. You should begin by making as extensive list as you can. You may find it helpful to pose the following questions to your research group:

1.   What do all dry cleaning establishments have in common?

2.   How do dry cleaning establishments differ from each other?

3.   What causes people to prefer one dry cleaner over another?

As each characteristic is discovered, you should consider whether that characteristic can be broken down into more specific items. For instance, if someone mentions "convenience," you might discuss whether there are different aspects of convenience, such as parking, business hours, and location.

A group discussion should help you generate an extensive list of possible product/service attributes. The next problem to be encountered is to keep the list down to a manageable number by elimination. You will do this by referring to the objectives of your study and by carefully considering which measures will be of interest to the client and/or which are likely to have the greatest decision value.

Listed below are five semantic differential scales that could be used to evaluate aspects of a retail store:

Poor Customer Service	1	2	3	4	5	6	Excellent Customer Service
Inconvenient Hours	1	2	3	4	5	6	Convenient Hours
High Prices	1	2	3	4	5	6	Low Prices
Poor Location	1	2	3	4	5	6	Good Location
Poor Specials	1	2	3	4	5	6	Valuable Specials

The above form of the semantic differential would most likely be used in a self-administered questionnaire in which the respondent would indicate his or her response by circling the appropriate number.

A modification of the above scale may be used when doing a telephone survey or in a personal interview when the interviewer reads the responses aloud. In these situations, the number of scale points must be kept small so that the respondent can remember them, usually about four and no more than five. Each question could be of the form:

> **Would you say that the customer service at Apex Dry Cleaning is excellent, good, fair, or poor?**

A five-point scale might add the response "outstanding" to the beginning of the scale or the response "unsatisfactory" to the end of the scale.

Using rating scales can become cumbersome. If you were to ask for the ratings of three products or services on five different attributes, this would require fifteen separate questions. A compact form for recording the responses to these types of questions is illustrated by Question 10 of Appendix 5A:

10.   Now I would like to read you some characteristics of dry cleaners. For each, I'd like you to tell me if that aspect of the dry cleaners is excellent, good, fair, or poor.

Would you say that the (CHARACTERISTIC BELOW) of (INSERT NAME) Dry Cleaning is (are) Excellent, Good, Fair, or Poor?

PROCEED THROUGH LIST OF ALL CHARACTERISTICS, FIRST FOR APEX, THEN FOR COMET AND FINALLY FOR ONE-HOUR. DO NOT START WITH THE SAME CHARACTERISTIC FROM THE LIST EACH TIME YOU GO THROUGH IT. AFTER RATING ALL THREE DRY CLEANERS, ASK THE FOLLOWING QUESTION FOR EACH CHARACTERISTIC AND RECORD THE RESPONSES IN THE FINAL SET OF COLUMNS.

I'd like to ask you about the importance of each of the characteristics in choosing a dry cleaners. First, I'd like to ask you about (READ CHARACTERISTIC FROM LIST). Would you say that (CHARACTERISTIC) is (are) Extremely Important, Very Important, Somewhat Important, or Not Important?

ITEM	RATING SCALES: 1 = EXCELLENT 2 = GOOD 3 = FAIR 4 = POOR	IMPORTANCE: 1 = EXTREMELY 2 = VERY 3 = SOMEWHAT 4 = NOT

ITEM	APEX	COMET	ONE HOUR	IMPORTANCE
Customer Service	1 2 3 4 (22)	1 2 3 4 (27)	1 2 3 4 (32)	1 2 3 4 (37)
Specials	1 2 3 4 (23)	1 2 3 4 (28)	1 2 3 4 (33)	1 2 3 4 (38)
Prices	1 2 3 4 (24)	1 2 3 4 (29)	1 2 3 4 (34)	1 2 3 4 (39)
Location	1 2 3 4 (25)	1 2 3 4 (30)	1 2 3 4 (35)	1 2 3 4 (40)
Hours	1 2 3 4 (26)	1 2 3 4 (31)	1 2 3 4 (36)	1 2 3 4 (41)

Note that the above set of questions actually contains two parts. First, each dry cleaning establishment is rated on all five characteristics. Then, the subject is asked about the importance of each characteristic. In Chapters Seven through Nine, we will explore the value of both of these types of information.

ANALYSIS METHODS

An important aspect of research design is the analysis that will ultimately be performed, and this will be strongly affected by the type of response format used. Many analysis techniques require data gathered with a high level of numerical precision. Calculation of means and standard deviations, as well as most other mathematical techniques, assume data gathered at least at the interval level. However, gathering highly detailed responses can be extremely burdensome on the respondent. As a general rule, the level of precision utilized should be at the highest level necessary for the analysis, and no higher. Often, the researcher who has not given serious consideration to the analysis phase is tempted to request detailed responses to every question. This will make the questionnaire longer, and each question will take more of the respondent's time and concentration.

For instance, consider the question regarding the respondent's income. If it were asked in an open-ended fashion, it would have implied that the interviewer wanted a specific dollar figure. It is rare that the research designer needs such precision. This places a burden on the respondent's memory and makes it more normative than it has to be. Consider the following alternate form of asking the question:

> **Please tell me your total family income from all sources before taxes in the past calendar year. Just read me the code from the card (HAND RESPONDENT CARD A).**

CARD A	
Less than $15,000	**CODE 1**
$15,001 to $25,000	**CODE 2**
$25,001 to $35,000	**CODE 3**
$35,001 to $45,000	**CODE 4**
$45,001 to $60,000	**CODE 5**
$60,001 to $100,000	**CODE 6**
Over $100,000	**CODE 7**

This categorical form of the income question has a couple of advantages. First, it saves time, because the interviewer does not have to read all of the categories. Second, since the respondent only picks a category, his or her exact income is not revealed. This perception is reinforced by the report of a code instead of a category. A well-trained interviewer will record the code in a detached manner, as though a CODE 2 is just as acceptable as a

CODE 6. Further the respondent knows that it may be nearly as likely that the respondent's income is at the top of the category as at the bottom.

The categorical form of measurement is widely used in marketing research when requesting numerical information from respondents. It can be used for such questions as age, purchase data in units or dollar amounts, and frequency of shopping. One caution is in order. When the categorical form is used, the top and bottom categories should be constructed such that a small percentage of the sample will fall into those groups. Later, in the analysis phase, the research designer may want to construct an estimate of the average income. In doing so, it will be necessary to estimate the average income of the respondents falling into each group. It would be reasonable to estimate that the average income of those choosing the category "$25,001 to $35,000" is around $30,000. However, what is the average income of those choosing the category "Over $100,000"? If this category represents a large proportion of the sample, whatever estimate is chosen will strongly influence the calculation of the average income.

Sometimes, the research designer is not interested in calculating averages. For instance, suppose the income question is to be used only to classify subjects into either a higher or a lower income group. In this case, the following question would be suitable:

I'd like to ask you about your total family income from all sources before taxes in the past calendar year. Would you say it was above or below $45,000?

Below $45,000 1
$45,000 or above 2
Refused or Don't Know 8

QUESTIONNAIRE MECHANICS

Use of a Word Processor. The layout of the questionnaire can be viewed as a sequential process. In fact, it is an iterative process of adding and deleting questions, revising the sequence of questions, and finally cleaning up the layout with interviewer instructions, precoding the questions, and numbering them. The modern word processor has greatly simplified the task of designing questionnaires. Revising the wording and adding interviewer instructions is easily done with insert and delete functions. All word processors also provide block operations that allow the movement of entire blocks of text (e.g., questions or groups of questions) from one point in the document to another.

If you do not use a word processor, you should design your questionnaire on index cards. Each question can be put on a separate card. After choosing which questions to retain and the wording of each, place the index cards in the desired order and type the questionnaire from these. In this manner, the questionnaire may be typed and numbered only once. If you use this approach, your instructor may allow you to turn in your index cards as your rough questionnaire. However, she or he will probably want to see a final copy of your questionnaire before you take it to the field.

Opener. The opener is the greeting that the interviewer will use when approaching a potential respondent. The opener must be brief yet persuasive enough to encourage the respondent's cooperation. You also want to provide enough information to convince the respondent that your reasons are legitimate. Many unethical sales approaches use the "cover" of marketing research to win cooperation. Here is an example of an opener for a student project conducted over the telephone (taken from Appendix 5A):

> **Hello, I'm (INTERVIEWER NAME), a student at (COLLEGE OR UNIVERSITY). Am I speaking to the male (female) head of the household?**
>
> > **(IF NO, ASK FOR APPROPRIATE PARTY AND PROCEED AGAIN WITH OPENER. IF A HEAD OF HOUSEHOLD IS NOT AVAILABLE, THANK RESPONDENT AND TERMINATE.)**
>
> **We are performing a student marketing research project on behalf of a local business. We are only interested in your opinions, and I will not try to sell you anything. Could I have about five minutes of your time? (IF NO, THANK RESPONDENT AND TERMINATE)**

The above opener can be modified in several ways. For instance, in an intercept interview (walking up to the respondent), it should be obvious that the respondent is an adult and is likely to be a head of household. If you are using random digit dialing, you might begin by asking if you have reached a business or a residence. There may be additional screening questions asked just after the greeting but prior to proceeding with the rest of the opener. One screening question might be a usage qualifier, such as:

> 1. **Do you use the services of a laundry or dry cleaners at least once in an average month? (IF NO THANK RESPONDENT AND TERMINATE)**

Another type of qualifier is a quota question. For instance, if you wanted a sample of eighty males and eighty females, you would record the sex of the respondent as soon as it is determined and terminate additional interviews with males or females once you had obtained eighty.

Funneling Technique. Questionnaire design uses a funneling technique, proceeding from general to specific questions. In addition, personal information and/or sensitive questions are usually placed toward the end of the interview to minimize respondent noncooperation. For instance, if income questions are asked early, respondents may wonder whether you are really doing legitimate marketing research or making a sales call. When placed at the end of the interview, after asking a number of "obvious" marketing research questions, the subject is less likely to feel threatened.

However, there are exceptions to the rule of proceeding from general to specific. For instance, if we were interested in unaided recall of brand names within a product category, we would want to ask this question prior to any mention of actual brands in other questions.

Instructions to Interviewers. It is desirable to place instructions directly on the questionnaire when an interviewer will be asking the questions. Most questionnaire designers use uppercase and lowercase letters for things that are actually read aloud, such as the text of each question and, when appropriate, the text of the answers. Instructions are provided to the interviewer in all-uppercase and interviewers are instructed to not read these instructions aloud (see the opener above for an example). If your word processor has the capability, you may choose to use **bold** or *italic* instead of all uppercase.

Skip Patterns. An important advantage of personal and telephone interviews is that the interviewer can guide the respondent through a complex questionnaire in a smooth, flowing manner. Below are three questions from Appendix 5A that illustrate a skip pattern.

6.   **Do you ever use dry cleaning coupons?**

(18)

YES 1
NO (SKIP TO QUESTION 8) 2
REFUSED OR DON'T KNOW (SKIP TO QUESTION 8) 8

7.   **When you use coupons, what one type do you most prefer? Would it be (READ LIST BELOW)**

(19)

Price discounts, such as $1 off and a $10 order 1
Special prices on suits 2
Special prices on slacks 3
Special prices on laundered shirts and blouses 4
REFUSED OR DON'T KNOW 8

8.   **Which dry cleaners do you use most often?**

Clearly, if the answer to Question Six is NO or REFUSED, it would be inappropriate to ask Question Seven. Thus, all uppercase instructions are provided to skip to Question Eight. Note also that the responses (e.g., YES and NO) are printed in all uppercase to indicate that the interviewer does not read those responses aloud, since they should be obvious to the subject.

Missing Values. There may be some responses that will be treated in the analysis phase as missing values. (The REFUSED OR DON'T KNOW responses above are examples.) For instance, you might want to know what portion of the sample uses Apex Dry Cleaners as a percentage of all the respondents who mentioned any dry cleaners. Thus, you want to leave REFUSED OR DON'T KNOW responses out of the divisor. It would be possible to leave missing responses off the questionnaire entirely. However, in the above example, since a REFUSED OR DON'T KNOW response is associated with a skip pattern, it should be included as a possible response.

Usually, there will only need to be one missing response for each answer. Occasionally, however, it may be desirable to have several. For instance, in the above example, we could have had one response for REFUSED and a separate response for DON'T KNOW. It is up to the research designer to decide if there is a good reason to tally the responses separately. For instance, if we were conducting a study on a sensitive topic, we might want to know how many people preferred not to answer the question, as well as how many did not know the answer. In Chapter Seven, we will introduce another missing value, NOT APPLICABLE, which could be added to the data set later through the use of computer editing.

The OTHER, SPECIFY Response. When unaided recall of brands is to be measured, the research designer may list most of the possible responses on the questionnaire. However, an OTHER, SPECIFY_____ response may be included to record unanticipated answers. Question Two of the Apex questionnaire illustrates the OTHER, SPECIFY response. If the respondent mentions any cleaners other than Apex, Comet, or One-Hour, the interviewer is to write out the name of the cleaners. Later, codes will be assigned to these other responses for entry into the computer. Note that it is not always necessary to provide an OTHER, SPECIFY response. If the research designer only wanted to know if the respondent had heard of Apex, Comet, One-Hour, or *any other brand*, then a simple response of OTHER would be sufficient.

Show Cards. When conducting interviews in person, the burden on the respondent can be minimized by placing some responses on index cards (called show cards) that may be handed to the respondent when the question is asked. The use of a show card was illustrated in the example income question discussed earlier.

Show cards may be used in a variety of ways. They may provide the responses to scaled questions, or they can be used to show respondents pictures of products or advertisements. Anytime it is desirable to expose the respondent to visual information, the use of show cards should be considered.

ADDITIONAL CONSIDERATIONS

Use a Separate Questionnaire for Each Respondent. Once your questionnaire is designed, typed in final form, thoroughly proofread, pretested, and revised, a separate questionnaire should be prepared for each respondent. Occasionally students will try to prepare only a small number of questionnaires, such as one for each interviewer, and record the responses directly on some type of coding form. If you try this, you will quickly discover your mistake. It is extremely cumbersome, slows down the interview, and is very prone to recording errors. Even if you are doing a telephone interview, in which the subject doesn't see the questionnaire, you will be well served to have a separate questionnaire for each completed interview. (An obvious exception would be if you are using Computer Assisted Telephone Interviewing - CATI - in which the questionnaire appears on the screen and responses are immediately recorded by the computer. This is discussed in your text.)

PRECODING

Preassigned Codes. You may have noticed that in the example questionnaire at the end of this chapter, the responses are followed by a dotted line at the end of which was a number. This provides a convenient place for the interviewer to record each response by circling the number. Note that some questions might have many possible responses, occasionally more than nine. In this case, the research designer must choose whether to use letters and numbers (providing up to thirty-six possible responses) or to use two-digit numbers. You will probably find that the use of two-digit numbers is a more desirable method. Although most computer programs have the ability to tabulate either letters or numbers, mixing letters and numbers can create difficult programming problems.

Preassigned Data Columns. In Chapter Seven, we will discuss data entry into the computer. Most computer programs assume that this data will be entered in the form of eighty column records. The record length of eighty is a throwback to the days when data was entered on punch cards. When entering data electronically, record lengths are much more flexible. However, since most computer screens display about eighty columns per line, the record length of eighty continues to be a standard. A single digit or alphabetic letter may be entered into each column of a record. If a single questionnaire requires more than eighty columns, multiple records may be used.

Another convention normally used to enter marketing research data is a fixed record format. This means the data from each question is entered into the same record column from each questionnaire. If data is missing from a certain question, the column is left blank. By using a fixed record format, it is not necessary to separate each item of data by blank spaces or other separation characters. This usually results in shorter record length and/or fewer records per respondent.

Often, it is desirable to place the record columns directly onto the questionnaire before it is printed (the small parenthesized numbers on the Apex questionnaire). Thus, each questionnaire will contain the data entry layout along with the response. This can speed and improve the accuracy of data entry. The difficulty is that once the questionnaires are printed, you will be committed to a data entry layout. Thus, it is extremely important to give careful consideration to data entry requirements when designing the questionnaire. In addition, some researchers feel that the presence of record columns on self-administered questionnaires "dehumanizes" the process, conveying an impression of the research study as a mechanical process rather than as a form of interpersonal communication. Consideration should be given to this argument versus the efficiencies gained by including record columns on the instrument.

In assigning record column numbers, it is important to consider both of the aspects of precoding mentioned above. If some questions will use codes higher than nine (that is, multiple digits) then a column must be left for each character. In addition, it may be difficult to determine in advance how many items will be coded from open-ended questions.

Appendix 5A contains the open-ended question:

4.   **What can you remember that the ads for Apex said or showed (PROBE AND RECORD FIRST TWO THINGS MENTIONED)?**

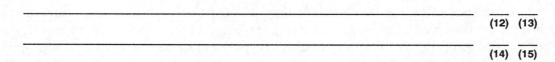

                                                                                (12)   (13)

                                                                                (14)   (15)

Two things should be noted from the above example. First, the research designers have decided in advance that two items of information will be coded from this question. In addition, it is believed that there will be more than ten different items mentioned in response to this question. Thus, the first item mentioned will coded as a two-digit number (e.g., 01, 02, 88, 99) and entered into columns 12 and 13. The second item mentioned will be coded into columns 14 and 15, also as a two-digit number.

When a question has only one possible response, the column assignment is a simple matter, as illustrated by the following question:

8.   **Which dry cleaners do you use most often?**

                                                                                (20)

APEX 1
COMET 2
ONE HOUR 3
OTHER SPECIFY_____ .... ____

The data from this question will be entered into column 20 of the data record.

Sometimes respondents are allowed to pick multiple responses to a single question:

3.   **What dry cleaners have you seen any advertisements for in the past month?**

APEX 1 (8)
COMET (SKIP TO QUESTION 5) 1 (9)
ONE HOUR (SKIP TO QUESTION 5) 1 (10)
OTHER SPECIFY_____ **(SKIP TO QUESTION 5)** .... ____ (11)
REFUSED OR DON'T KNOW (SKIP TO QUESTION 5)

Note that if a respondent mentions more than one brand it would be difficult to enter more than one code into a single column. In fact, this question should be thought of as four questions: "Have you seen advertising for Apex?" "Have you seen advertising for Comet?" and so on. In the above example, the awareness or nonawareness of each of the cleaners is entered into columns 8, 9, 10, and 11 by entering the coded value 1 or leaving it blank if the brand was not mentioned. The OTHER, SPECIFY response allows codes to be assigned later to additional brands that were mentioned.

Remember: If there is only one response to a question, you only need one column (or set of columns if using two-digit codes). If there is more than one response to a question, you need to assign a column to each response.

PRETEST

It is essential that you pretest your questionnaire prior to final printing. It is rare that a pretest does not reveal some problems with the questionnaire. Some of the problems that might be uncovered by a pretest include:

1. Question wording and/or possible misinterpretation

2. Responses that have been omitted

3. Sequencing of questions

4. Skip patterns

5. Incomplete instructions for interviewers

You should pretest your questionnaire on at least ten to fifteen respondents. You should use the same procedures and methodology you intend to use in your study. For example, choose pretest subjects in the same way as you will choose your sample, and do not pretest a telephone interview in a personal interview setting.

If the changes suggested by the pretest are minor, it is probably safe to proceed after these changes are made. However, if the pretest suggests major changes in the questionnaire, a second round of pretesting should be performed.

APPENDIX 5A
SAMPLE QUESTIONNAIRE

DRY CLEANERS STUDY   INTERVIEW ID   ___ ___ ___
                                                              (1) (2) (3)

Hello, I'm (INTERVIEWER NAME), a student at (COLLEGE OR UNIVERSITY). Am I speaking to the male (female) head of the household?

> (IF NO, ASK FOR APPROPRIATE PARTY AND PROCEED AGAIN WITH OPENER. IF THE MALE OR FEMALE HEAD OF HOUSEHOLD IS NOT AVAILABLE, THANK RESPONDENT AND TERMINATE.)

We are performing a student marketing research project on behalf of a local business. We are only interested in your opinions, and I will not try to sell you anything. Could I have about five minutes of your time (IF NO, THANK RESPONDENT AND TERMINATE)?

1.   Do you use the services of a laundry or dry cleaners at least once in an average month? (IF NO THANK RESPONDENT AND TERMINATE)

2.   When you think of dry cleaning establishments, which ones come to mind?

> IF APEX, COMET, OR ONE HOUR MENTIONED, RECORD UNDER UNAIDED RECALL. IF OTHER BRANDS MENTIONED, RECORD FIRST ONE MENTIONED UNDER OTHER SPECIFY.

> IF APEX, COMET, OR ONE HOUR NOT MENTIONED, ASK, FOR EACH,

Have you also heard of (name of establishment) Dry Cleaning? (RECORD UNDER AIDED RECALL)

	UNAIDED RECALL	AIDED RECALL	
APEX	1	2	(4)
COMET	1	2	(5)
ONE HOUR	1	2	(6)
OTHER SPECIFY_____	1	2	(7)
REFUSED OR DON'T KNOW			

3.   What dry cleaners have you seen any advertisements for in the past month?

APEX	1	(8)
COMET (SKIP TO QUESTION 5)	1	(9)
ONE HOUR (SKIP TO QUESTION 5)	1	(10)
OTHER SPECIFY_____ (SKIP TO QUESTION 5) .... ____		(11)
REFUSED OR DON'T KNOW (SKIP TO QUESTION 5)		

4. What can you remember that the ads for Apex said or showed (PROBE AND RECORD FIRST TWO THINGS MENTIONED)?

_____   ___ ___
                                                    (12) (13)

_____   ___ ___
                                                    (14) (15)

5. How much, in an average month, do you spend on <u>dry cleaning</u> service for your household? Please do not include laundry. (RECORD INTO ONE OF THE FOLLOWING CATEGORIES)

5A. How much, in an average month, do you spend on <u>laundry</u> service for your household? (RECORD INTO ONE OF THE FOLLOWING CATEGORIES)

	DRY CLEANING (16)	LAUNDRY (17)
LESS THAN $10.00	1	1
$11 TO $20	2	2
$21 TO $35	3	3
$36 TO $50	4	4
$51 TO $75	5	5
$76 to $100	6	6
More than $100	7	7
REFUSED ON DON'T KNOW	8	8

6. Do you ever use laundry or dry cleaning coupons?   (18)
   YES 1
   NO (SKIP TO QUESTION 8) 2
   REFUSED OR DON'T KNOW (SKIP TO QUESTION 8) 8

7. When you use coupons, what one type do you most prefer. Would it be (READ LIST BELOW)?
                                                                             (19)
   Price discounts, such as $ 1 off on a $ 10 order 1
   Special prices on suits 2
   Special prices on slacks 3
   Special prices on laundered shirts and blouses 4
   REFUSED OR DON'T KNOW 8

8. Which dry cleaners do you use most often?
                                                                             (20)
   APEX 1
   COMET 2
   ONE HOUR 3
   OTHER SPECIFY_____ .... ___
   REFUSED OR DON'T KNOW 8

9. Approximately how far is Apex Dry Cleaners from your home? (PLACE RESPONSE INTO ONE OF THE FOLLOWING CATEGORIES)
                                                                             (21)
   LESS THAN ONE MILE 1
   ONE MILE OR MORE BUT LESS THAN TWO MILES 2
   TWO MILES OR MORE BUT LESS THAN THREE MILES 3
   THREE MILES OR MORE BUT LESS THAN FIVE MILES 4
   FIVE MILES OR MORE 5
   REFUSED OR DON'T KNOW 8

10. Now I would like to read you some characteristics of dry cleaners. For each, I'd like you to tell me if that aspect of the dry cleaners is excellent, good, fair, or poor.

Would you say that the (CHARACTERISTIC BELOW) of (INSERT NAME) Dry Cleaning is (are) Excellent, Good, Fair, or Poor?

> PROCEED THROUGH LIST OF ALL CHARACTERISTICS, FIRST FOR APEX, THEN FOR COMET AND FINALLY FOR ONE HOUR. DO NOT START WITH THE SAME CHARACTERISTIC FROM THE LIST EACH TIME YOU GO THROUGH IT. AFTER RATING ALL THREE DRY CLEANERS ASK THE FOLLOWING QUESTION FOR EACH CHARACTERISTIC AND RECORD THE RESPONSES IN THE FINAL SET OF COLUMNS.

I'd like to ask you about the importance of each of the characteristics in choosing a dry cleaners. First, I'd like to ask you about (READ CHARACTERISTIC FROM LIST). Would you say that (CHARACTERISTIC) is (are) Extremely Important, Very Important, Somewhat Important, or Not Important?

ITEM	RATING SCALES: 1 = EXCELLENT 2 = GOOD 3 = FAIR 4 = POOR	IMPORTANCE: 1 = EXTREMELY 2 = VERY 3 = SOMEWHAT 4 = NOT

	APEX	COMET	ONE HOUR	IMPORTANCE
Customer Service	1 2 3 4 (22)	1 2 3 4 (27)	1 2 3 4 (32)	1 2 3 4 (37)
Specials	1 2 3 4 (23)	1 2 3 4 (28)	1 2 3 4 (33)	1 2 3 4 (38)
Prices	1 2 3 4 (24)	1 2 3 4 (29)	1 2 3 4 (34)	1 2 3 4 (39)
Location	1 2 3 4 (25)	1 2 3 4 (30)	1 2 3 4 (35)	1 2 3 4 (40)
Hours	1 2 3 4 (26)	1 2 3 4 (31)	1 2 3 4 (36)	1 2 3 4 (41)

CLASSIFICATION QUESTIONS

Now I'd like to ask you a few questions for classification purposes only.

11. RECORD, BASED UPON THE OPENER. RESPONDENT IS: (42)
   MALE 1
   FEMALE 2

12. Which of the following categories includes your age? Are you (READ LIST)

(43)

Under 21	1
21 to 25	2
26 to 35	3
36 to 49	4
50 to 69	5
70 older	6
REFUSED OR DON'T KNOW	8

13. What is your marital status? Are you (CODE INTO ONE OF THE FOLLOWING CATEGORIES)

(44)

Single	1
Married	2
Separated, Divorced or Widowed	3
REFUSED OR DON'T KNOW	8

14. How many members are there in your household, including yourself? (RECORD NUMBER IN SPACE PROVIDED. IF NINE OR MORE, RECORD THE NUMBER 9. IF REFUSED, LEAVE BLANK).

___
(45)

15. What is your occupation?

_____

___
(46)

16. Which of the following categories includes your total family income during the last calendar year from all sources before taxes? (READ LIST)

(47)

$15,000 or under	1
$15,001 to $25,000	2
$25,001 to $40,000	3
$40,001 to $60,000	5
$60,001 to $100,000	6
Over $100,000	7
REFUSED OR DON'T KNOW	8

RECORD RESPONDENT'S PHONE NUMBER   __ __ __   __ __ __ __

That completes our interview. Thank you very much for your time and cooperation.

CHAPTER SIX
SAMPLING AND SAMPLE SIZE DETERMINATION

INTRODUCTION

The purpose of sampling is to generate measures that will be representative of a population of interest. To a great extent, the quality of your results will depend upon the quality of your sample. Poor sampling procedures can be a large source of error in marketing research studies.

CENSUS VERSUS SAMPLE

The first issue in sampling is to define the population. The population (also referred to as the universe) is the group to which the results of the sample will be generalized. Occasionally, when the population is small, the researcher may choose to use a census rather than a sample. A census is a complete inclusion of all the members of the population in the research study. A census might be appropriate if, for instance, you were conducting a survey among the members of the marketing club at your university. However, when the population is large, a sample will usually be chosen because it would be faster and cheaper than doing a census.

PROBABILITY VERSUS NONPROBABILITY SAMPLES

Probability Samples. Sampling methods fall into two categories, probability and nonprobability. Probability samples use random methods to select members. In a probability sample, each member of the population has a known nonzero chance of being included in the sample. Whether a member of the population is included in the sample will depend upon the laws of statistical probability. Probability methods allow the researcher to use the results of the sample to represent the population within some estimated degree of error.

On the other hand, nonprobability samples allow considerable researcher discretion in choosing members of the sample. For this reason, some members of the population may be systematically excluded (and thus have zero chance of being selected). Table 6.1 breaks down some important types of probability and non-probability samples.

TABLE 6.1
TYPES OF SAMPLES

Probability Samples	NonProbability Samples
Simple Random	Convenience
Systematic	Quota
Stratified	Judgment
Cluster	

Simple Random Samples. A simple random sample is one in which all members of the population have an equal (nonzero) probability of being included. The sampling elements are selected from a sampling frame, a listing that is believed to provide a complete enumeration of all the members of the population. For instance, a list provided by the registrar could provide a good sampling frame for a student population.

To perform the simple random sample:

1. Define the population.

2. Obtain a sampling frame, an exhaustive list of all of the members of the population.

3. Randomly select the desired number of sampling elements from the sampling frame.

4. Take the measures of interest from each sampling element.

If the above requirements are met, the only source of error caused by the sampling itself would be random sampling error, the size of which may be estimated through various sampling formulas. However, the above requirements suggest that it is nearly impossible to develop a perfect sample for a marketing research study. Once the population has been defined, it is always difficult to locate a sampling frame that does not eliminate some members of the population. For example, the student telephone directory is notoriously out-of-date at most universities. One student study, conducted at a major university, indicated that over one-third of the numbers were in error. For another example, suppose the population were defined as all households within a city. Frame error would occur if the study were conducted over the telephone, since some households do not have phones and would not be included in any possible telephone sampling frame.

Failure to perform the fourth requirement above is, sometimes, a very large source of error in marketing research studies. Major deviations from the requirements of simple random samples (as well as other probability types) are associated with noncontact and nonresponse. These types of errors are referred to as nonsampling errors. Of the numbers selected for inclusion in the sampling frame, many people will not be at home (noncontact). Of those who are at home, many will refuse to cooperate at all, and others may refuse to answer some of the questions (nonresponse). Frame error, noncontact error and nonresponse error are all examples of nonsampling errors that may occur in any type of sample.

Stratified Samples. Another common type of probability sample is the stratified sample. This type of sample is very much like the simple random sample. However, some restrictions are imposed to ensure that a fixed number of sampling elements are included in two or more groups. There are two types of stratified samples, proportional, and non-proportional.

Proportional stratified samples attempt to provide *proper* representation of various groups in the sample. For example, if it were known that the population of students included 28 percent freshman, 26 percent sophomores, 24 percent juniors and 22 percent seniors, a sample of 200 students would include 56, 52, 48, and 44 students in the respective groups.

The nonproportional stratified sample attempts to achieve *adequate* representation of important groups of interest to the research designer. The accuracy of a sampling estimate depends upon the sample size as well as the degree of variability of what is to be measured. Sometimes this variability will not be equal within all groups of the population. For instance, buyers of a product may be concentrated primarily among a group of high-income consumers. On the other hand, nonbuyers may be widely dispersed throughout the income distribution. Thus, the variability of income in the group of buyers is smaller than the variability of income of nonbuyers. This variability will have an impact on sampling accuracy. If an equal size sample were taken from each group, more accurate estimates would be obtainable from the group with smaller variability. This may be compensated for by selecting larger samples from those groups with a greater degree of variability. Of course, this presents a difficulty for the research designer in that this variability must be estimated in advance of determining the sample size.

Cluster Samples. A cluster sample is often used when a personal interview is desired and the sample is to be selected from a geographic area. If two hundred households were randomly selected throughout the city, extensive interviewer travel time and cost would be incurred. An alternative is a cluster sample. In this method, you might first randomly choose city blocks (clusters of the population) throughout the city. This could be done by overlaying a numbered grid on a city map, randomly selecting grid intersections, and choosing the city block closest to the selected grid locations. On each block, interviewers would use random methods to choose, say, five households from that block. Thus, there would be only forty travel destinations instead of two hundred, enhancing the economic efficiency of the sampling method.

NonProbability Samples. Nonprobability samples are often substituted for probability samples when resources are severely limited or when some goal of the researcher is more likely to be accomplished by nonrandom selection methods. It is common when recruiting focus group members to select people who are especially heavy users of a product category. While these people may not be representative of the target market, they may provide for a more productive focus group. For instance, in a focus group for lawn fertilizer, we might restrict the sample to people who have purchased at least three bags of fertilizer in the past year, even though the average homeowner may purchase less than two bags. If the purpose of the focus group is to explore how consumers make brand choices of fertilizer, it may not be desirable to include infrequent purchasers. This type of sample is often referred to as a judgment sample.

Another nonprobability sampling method is the convenience sample. In this method, the researcher uses any convenient method to recruit a sample of the desired size. For instance, the interviewers might be directed to station themselves at a strategic location in the student union building and interview anyone who happens by until twenty interviews are completed. Clearly, any student's chance of being selected depends upon the probability of his or her walking past that point at the time the interviewing is taking place. This probability is likely to differ widely among students. For some, who spend little time in the student union building, it may be near zero.

A third nonprobability sampling method is quota sampling. The establishment of quotas is often utilized to compensate for the deficiencies of nonprobability samples. For instance, consider the convenience sample described above. In order to make the sample *appear* more representative, the researcher might establish quotas of freshmen, sophomores, juniors, and seniors. A further quota of 50 percent males and 50 percent females could be established. The goal in this situation is similar to the goal of proportional stratified sampling discussed earlier. Nevertheless, the imposition of quotas cannot account for the fact that some students rarely come into the student union building. Thus, the sample cannot be considered a probability sample.

Quota samples may also be used in ways similar to nonproportional stratified sampling. Suppose it is believed that about 10 percent of the households in the target market are customers of Apex Dry Cleaning. A random telephone sample of 200 households would be expected to generate about 20 customers and 180 noncustomers. The sampling formulas (discussed later) suggest that the sampling error in the small group will be much larger than the sampling error in the large group. For this reason, the research design might specify that the sample will include 100 customers and 100 noncustomers. This necessitates an initial screening question regarding patronage at Apex. After 100 noncustomers have been interviewed, additional noncustomers will be rejected until the required number of 100 customers has been contacted. One problem with nonproportional quota and stratified samples is that all resulting statistics for the combined sample must be corrected to account for the fact that the incidence of certain groups in the sample may differ from their actual incidence in the population.

It is up to the researcher to recognize the deficiencies of samples that use nonprobability selection methods. This is particularly true in the case of quota samples. If quotas are imposed primarily to compensate for deficiencies caused by convenience or judgment in selecting members of the sample, the quotas may do little more than force the sample to *appear* to be representative of the population, even when it is not. However, if the research designer specifies random methods of selection, imposing quotas only to ensure that the sizes of the various groups are sufficient to accomplish the research objectives, the resulting quota sample will more closely resemble the probability samples discussed earlier.

Convenience and judgment samples (as well as quota samples based upon convenience and/or judgment) may be deficient in a number of ways:

1. Statistical sampling formulas (which assume random selection) do not strictly apply. Estimates based upon these samples may contain substantial amounts of undetected bias.

2. Ensuring representation on one characteristic does not provide representativeness on others. In the convenience sample conducted in the student union building, it is very likely that students who live off campus would be underrepresented.

3. It may be very difficult, if not impossible, to check on the representativeness of the sample except by comparison with the population characteristics. These, of course, may be unknown.

4. Nonprobability samples often allow a great deal of interviewer discretion in selecting members of the sample, and this can cause seriously biased estimates of population values. For example, it is common for extroverted interviewers to oversample from members of the opposite sex and for shy interviewers to avoid them.

SAMPLING FROM LISTS

Simple Random Sampling. It is common to choose sample members from lists when conducting a telephone interview or mail survey. These lists become the sampling frame. Researchers might use the current student directory or a list obtained from the registrar when conducting a student survey. Commercial marketing research companies often select samples from lists obtained from list brokers.

Selecting from lists can be done using the simple random sample procedures discussed earlier. Suppose we have a listing of the 22,000 students enrolled in a university. We can assign a consecutive number to each name on the list. Next, random numbers in the interval from 1 to 22,000 would be generated. A number of names would be selected to yield a sample of sufficient size to conduct the study. If the desired final sample size were 150, it might be necessary to obtain several times this many sample members to account for not-at-homes, refusals and disconnected numbers.

Systematic Sampling. A less cumbersome method of sampling from lists is to use systematic sampling. Systematic sampling is not truly a random method; however, for most marketing research purposes, the sample generated should not be deficient, compared to a true random sample. In systematic sampling, random methods are used to generate the first few selections, and then a system is used to generate the remainder.

The following method can be used for generating a student sample from a seventy page directory that will be used by six interviewers:

1. Calculate the skip interval by dividing the number of pages in the directory by the number of interviewers. Keep the integer portion of the result ($X = 70/6 = 11.7 = 11$)

2. From a table of random numbers, or using a random number generator, choose a random number in the interval 1 to 7 (one greater than the number of interviewers). Use this number to select the first page to be used. Select subsequent pages by adding the skip interval, X, from Step 1 to the number of the page selected (e.g., if the random number is 2, then select page 2, 13, 24, 35, etc).

3. Each interviewer will select sampling elements from the page by first selecting two random numbers in some interval, such as between 1 and 10 (for example, let's use the numbers 3 and 8). Using the first of these two numbers, the interviewer will select the third name on the page. The next name will be the eighth name following the first name selected. The next name would again add the interval 8, resulting in a choice of the nineteenth name on the page, and so on.

It is important that whatever system is established, it be followed strictly to avoid bias in selection. There is sometimes a tendency on the part of interviewers to systematically skip over some names, for instance, those that might be hard to pronounce, or are of obvious ethnic origin (presenting possible language difficulties).

A problem that occasionally occurs with systematic sampling is if the list contains a regularly repeating pattern. For instance, suppose we wanted to take a sample from a list containing daily sales in a store. If the skip interval were seven, then all of data in the sample would come from the same day of the week. Lists of names listed in alphabetical order are not likely to contain such regularly repeating patterns, as long as sampling is not confined to specific parts of the list, for example only names beginning with the letters A or B.

RANDOM DIGIT DIALING

Random digit dialing is a technique for selecting telephone numbers from all possible telephone numbers through a random method of selection. The purest form of random digit dialing would simply generate a 10-digit random number and use it as the sampled number. Unfortunately, of all the possible 10-digit numbers in the United States, only about 1 in 170 represent actual working numbers. In order to make the process more efficient, the researcher should screen out all 10-digit numbers that are not in one of the 103 working area codes and approximately 30,000 working exchanges. This method requires obtaining information on working area codes and exchanges within the geographical area that contains the population. This is practical for large marketing research companies that conduct hundreds of telephone studies per year. It would be highly impractical for a small student project, such as the one you are conducting.

Therefore, one alternative to pure random digit dialing is the plus-one (also know as the add-a-digit) method. In this method, the telephone directory is used as a sampling frame, and telephone numbers are randomly selected (see the earlier section on systematic sampling for information about sampling from lists). To each selected number a "1" is added. Thus, 555-123$\underline{4}$ becomes 555-123$\underline{5}$. In addition to being easy to use, this method has several practical benefits:

1. The telephone directory provides a readily available sampling frame.

2. Unlisted telephone numbers have a chance of being included.

3. The numbers selected come from working exchanges and are concentrated among banks of numbers that have actually been activated by the telephone company.

4. Exchanges will be sampled in closer proportion to the number of working numbers in the exchange.

The method also has a few disadvantages:

1. If business and residence numbers are assigned from the same exchanges, many of the generated numbers will be businesses, even if the original numbers came from the residence pages (this problem applies as well to other methods of random digit dialing).

2.   In geographical areas where the directories are out of date or where the population is growing rapidly, recently added exchanges may be excluded from the sample or not sampled in the proper proportions. Depending upon the definition of the population and the objectives of the study, this should be considered as a possible limitation of the method.

This method would probably not be acceptable if the population were "all students enrolled in the university" and the student directory were used a sampling frame. Unless student numbers all belong to the same exchange, or are at least assigned in blocks from working exchanges, the number resulting from adding a digit could just as easily be a nonstudent number.

INTERCEPT INTERVIEWING

Intercept interviewing is widely used in marketing research, even though it is clearly a form of nonprobability sampling. Often, the accomplishment of the research objectives calls for a personal interview because the interview is lengthy or requires the use of visual materials. Until the 1960s, most personal interviewing was conducted door-to-door. However, in recent years, because of rising costs and growing concerns about personal safety, the marketing research industry has sought other ways of gathering data. Despite its obvious limitations, intercept interviewing (often done in shopping malls) has largely replaced the door-to-door method as the preferred way of conducting interviews when face-to-face contact is required.

Student projects often use intercept interviewing. For instance, in gathering a sample of the student population, interviewers might be stationed at locations throughout the campus at various times of the day. When it is desirable to interview customers of a business, interviewers may conduct the interview on the client's premises. Some things to consider in designing a method of intercept interviewing include:

1.   If interviewing at more than one site, choose locations so that a broad cross-section of the population will be included.

2.   Do not conduct all interviews at the same time of the day or on the same day of the week.

3.   Interviewers should use a random selection procedure, such as intercepting every fifth person who walks by. This eliminates some of the selection bias that interviewers often inject into the study by interviewing members of only one sex, approaching only those people who do not appear to be in a hurry, or who look especially compliant and cooperative.

CALLBACK PROCEDURES

If you use telephone interviewing, consideration should be given to using a callback procedure. As each number is dialed, the outcome of the attempt should be recorded on a call record sheet. An example of a call record sheet is contained in Appendix 6A. Beside each number attempted annotations are made to indicate a completed interview (C), a busy signal (BY), a nonworking number (NW), a not-at-home (NAH), a refusal (R), or a request to call back later (CB).

You may choose to make one or more callbacks to those numbers that are busy or not-at-home. Depending upon the objectives of the study, undersampling from these households could inject considerable bias into the results. For instance, if you are conducting a study of people's leisure time activities, you would not want to systematically under-represent those who are spending their time away from home. It is common to see commercial research studies specifying as many as five or more callbacks to avoid excluding busy and not-at-home numbers. It is up to the research designer to determine whether a callback procedure should be used to minimize the bias that can be injected by leaving out busy or not-at-home numbers.

ADDITIONAL CONSIDERATIONS IN CHOOSING SAMPLING METHODS

As you can see, some sampling procedures can be cumbersome and time-consuming. For this reason, your instructor may allow you considerable latitude in choosing methods of obtaining your sample. Nonprobability methods may be considered acceptable as long as you carefully explain the limitations of the method you choose. For instance, it is common for project groups to obtain the permission of the instructor to distribute brief questionnaires before, after, or even during class hours. From the previous discussion, a number of deficiencies of this method should be apparent to you. You should comment in your research report on the kinds of biases that might have occurred as a result of your sampling methods.

SAMPLE SIZE DETERMINATION

The size of the sample is an important factor that affects the accuracy of your survey. Other things being equal, larger samples will provide more accurate estimates of the population values of interest. Ideally, the size of the sample should be based upon some prespecified level of accuracy required to accomplish the research objectives. As a practical matter, sample sizes are often set by the constraints of the research budget or other resource restrictions. This may be the case in your study. However, your instructor may expect you, in your research proposal or report, to go through the exercise of specifying some desired level of accuracy and determining the sample size required to obtain it. Having done this, you may be allowed to invoke resource constraints to justify the smaller size sample you will actually use.

Sampling is the basis for the entire study of statistics. The area of sampling, sample size determination, and sampling accuracy fills entire textbooks. In this section, we will present some basic sampling formulas that you will find useful. Your marketing research text will provide a more complete treatment.

Sampling Accuracy of a Mean Value. The following formula may be used for determining the required sample size when an *average value* is to be estimated within some desired level of precision.

$$n = \frac{Z^2 \sigma^2}{C^2}$$

where: n = required sample size.
          Z = desired level of confidence.
          σ = assumed standard deviation of value to be estimated.
          C = maximum allowable error.

In using the equation, the research designer must first decide upon the desired level of confidence (e.g., 95 percent) and find the corresponding Z value in a table of the standard normal distribution. Next, it is necessary to specify some assumed standard deviation (σ) of the quantity to be estimated. This requires some speculation since we are determining the sample size in advance of actually gathering the data. The estimate can come from a variety of sources. For instance, if the quantity estimated is descriptive information, such as average age or average income, we can consult the most recent update of the *Census of Population*. Another source may be a previous survey or a trade publication that may have estimated the quantity for other reasons. Trade associations often conduct surveys of their target audience and publish the results. Lacking any external source, the researcher may have to fall back on judgment or a pilot study.

Finally, it is necessary to specify some maximum error (C) to be allowed in estimating the quantity.

Example:

Suppose the researchers were interested in estimating the average amount spent on dry cleaning per month for the population. They want to be 90 percent confident that the result will be within two dollars of the true mean value for the population. The Z value is easily determined to be 1.64 from a table of the normal distribution. Where might the standard deviation come from? If an old survey or trade association data were not available, it might be necessary to estimate this quantity. One way to do this is to try to estimate the maximum and minimum that most individuals would spend on dry cleaning per month. We can pose the following hypothetical question:

"What might be an upper and a lower boundary of monthly dry cleaning spending that would include 95 percent of the population."

Suppose that we believe that only about 5 percent of the population would spend less than $5 or more than $100 per month. You should recall from your statistics course that, in a normally distributed population, 95 percent of the population will lie within plus or minus 1.96 standard deviations. Thus, the width of this 95 percent interval is 3.92 standard deviations (2 x 1.96). Therefore, 3.92 standard deviations corresponds to the interval of $95 ($100 - $5.00) we described above. We can estimate one standard deviation as:

$$\sigma = \frac{\$95}{3.92} = \$24.23$$

We now have all the necessary information to determine the required sample size.

$$n = \frac{1.64^2 \; 24.23^2}{\$2.00^2} = 394.76$$

which we would round off to 395 since it is not possible to interview   .76 of one respondent.

Sampling Accuracy for Estimating Proportions. The following formula is widely used for determining the size of the sample required to achieve a prespecified level of accuracy on a question designed to estimate a population *proportion*. Proportion questions will only have two possible responses, such as yes/no or aware of brand/not aware of brand.

$$n = \frac{Z^2 P(1-P)}{C^2}$$

where:
n	=	required sample size
Z	=	desired level of confidence
P	=	expected proportion
C	=	maximum allowable error

In using the above equation, the researcher must specify the desired level of confidence in the results (e.g., 95 percent) and find the corresponding Z value in a table of the normal distribution. The expected proportion (P) must also be provided. Remember, this is done in advance of gathering the data, so it will be necessary to estimate it. In addition, you must specify the maximum allowable error (C) you will allow in estimating this proportion.

Example:
You want to estimate the proportion of the population who have patronized Apex Dry Cleaning at least once in the past year. Suppose you expect the percentage to be around 20 percent. Thus, the estimated proportion is .2 (which may turn out to differ from the results you actually obtain from your survey). The objectives of your survey suggest that the estimate of the proportion should be within plus or minus five percent of the true proportion. Therefore, C would be .05. For a desired level of confidence of 95 percent (Z = 1.96), the calculated sample size would be:

$$n = \frac{1.96^2\ .2\ (1-.2)}{.05^2} = 245.86$$

which we would round off to 246.

A General Sample Size Formula. If there were one key question within the survey on which a desired level of accuracy must be achieved, one of the two methods described above would be utilized. The choice would depend upon whether the key question involved a mean or a proportion. Having done this, the accuracy on the remaining questions is allowed to fall where it may. If the study contains no such key question, the researcher may strive for some general level of overall accuracy. This may be accomplished by using the formula for determining the accuracy of a proportion in a special way.

Note that in the proportion formula, we find the term [P (1 - P)], where P is the assumed proportion. This term reaches a maximum when P is equal to .5 (.eg., .5 x (1 - .5) =.25). Any value of P smaller than .5 would result in a lower value (e.g., .4 x (1 - .4) = .24). Since this term is in the numerator of the formula, any value of P other than .5 would call for a smaller sample size. The largest sample size will always be generated by using a value of P equal to .5, and the resulting sample size will provide at least the desired level of accuracy or better. In the Apex example this would call for a sample size of:

$$n = \frac{1.96^2\ .5\ (1-.5)}{.05^2} = 384.16$$

which we would round off to 385.

APPENDIX 6A
CALL RECORD SHEET FOR TELEPHONE INTERVIEWING

CODES FOR CALL OUTCOMES:

C	Completed Interview		CB	Call Back (Note time and date)
NW	Not a Working Number		Q	Quota Exhausted
BY	Busy Number		S	Failed Screening Questions
NAH	Not at Home		R	Refused Interview

TELEPHONE NUMBER	CALL OUTCOME	SUPERVISOR INITIALS
_____	_____	_____
_____	_____	_____
_____	_____	_____
_____	_____	_____
_____	_____	_____
_____	_____	_____
_____	_____	_____
_____	_____	_____
_____	_____	_____
_____	_____	_____
_____	_____	_____
_____	_____	_____
_____	_____	_____
_____	_____	_____
_____	_____	_____
_____	_____	_____
_____	_____	_____

CALL RECORD SHEET FOR TELEPHONE INTERVIEWING

CODES FOR CALL OUTCOMES:

C	Completed Interview	CB	Call Back (Note time and date)
NW	Not a Working Number	Q	Quota Exhausted
BY	Busy Number	S	Failed Screening Questions
NAH	Not at Home	R	Refused Interview

TELEPHONE NUMBER	CALL OUTCOME	SUPERVISOR INITIALS
_____	_____	_____
_____	_____	_____
_____	_____	_____
_____	_____	_____
_____	_____	_____
_____	_____	_____
_____	_____	_____
_____	_____	_____
_____	_____	_____
_____	_____	_____
_____	_____	_____
_____	_____	_____
_____	_____	_____
_____	_____	_____
_____	_____	_____
_____	_____	_____
_____	_____	_____
_____	_____	_____

CALL RECORD SHEET FOR TELEPHONE INTERVIEWING

CODES FOR CALL OUTCOMES:

C	Completed Interview	CB	Call Back (Note time and date)
NW	Not a Working Number	Q	Quota Exhausted
BY	Busy Number	S	Failed Screening Questions
NAH	Not at Home	R	Refused Interview

TELEPHONE NUMBER	CALL OUTCOME	SUPERVISOR INITIALS
_____	_____	_____
_____	_____	_____
_____	_____	_____
_____	_____	_____
_____	_____	_____
_____	_____	_____
_____	_____	_____
_____	_____	_____
_____	_____	_____
_____	_____	_____
_____	_____	_____
_____	_____	_____
_____	_____	_____
_____	_____	_____
_____	_____	_____
_____	_____	_____

CALL RECORD SHEET FOR TELEPHONE INTERVIEWING

CODES FOR CALL OUTCOMES:

C	Completed Interview	CB	Call Back (Note time and date)
NW	Not a Working Number	Q	Quota Exhausted
BY	Busy Number	S	Failed Screening Questions
NAH	Not at Home	R	Refused Interview

TELEPHONE NUMBER	CALL OUTCOME	SUPERVISOR INITIALS
_____	_____	_____
_____	_____	_____
_____	_____	_____
_____	_____	_____
_____	_____	_____
_____	_____	_____
_____	_____	_____
_____	_____	_____
_____	_____	_____
_____	_____	_____
_____	_____	_____
_____	_____	_____
_____	_____	_____
_____	_____	_____
_____	_____	_____
_____	_____	_____
_____	_____	_____

CHAPTER SEVEN
DATA COLLECTION AND TABULATION

DATA COLLECTION

Once your sampling procedures have been determined and your questionnaire developed and pretested, you are ready to begin collecting data. Regardless of the data collection method, you should always have a separate questionnaire for each subject. Each interviewer should perform several practice interviews on members of the group, and perhaps on friends or members of other groups, before actually conducting interviews in the field.

Collecting and Tallying Completed Interviews. One group member should be assigned to collect the interviews. These must be turned in as soon as possible after they are completed. You may want to have each member of the group complete five interviews and turn them in prior to proceeding with the remainder of the data gathering.

The person collecting the completed interviews will have several responsibilities:

1. As they are turned in, questionnaires should be assigned an identifying code, typically a three-digit number.

2. If you are using a stratified sample or quota, the person collecting the data must keep track of the number of responses in each category and advise the other group members if any quotas have been filled.

3. Carefully screen each questionnaire shortly after it is turned in. Screening requires that:

    a. each questionnaire is checked to ensure that all instructions were followed, especially skip patterns. Occasionally, the person doing the screening will notice something that interviewers are doing incorrectly and will want to call all of the interviewers to correct this.

    b. each questionnaire must be checked for completeness. It may not be necessary that every question be answered if there are skip patterns. On the other hand, there may be several key questions that are critical for accomplishing the research objectives. Failure to obtain answers to these questions would result in discarding the entire questionnaire.

    c. questionnaires are checked for internal consistency. For instance, if a person says that he or she has not purchased the product, we would not expect a question about the number of units purchased to be answered.

CODING

What Is Coding? It would be impractical to enter all of the information from open-ended responses into the computer data set. Thus, it will be necessary to classify these responses into groups and to assign identifying numeric or alphabetic codes that will be entered into the data set.

Coding should not begin, in very large surveys, until after all of the questionnaires have been completed. Sometimes answers to questionnaires turned in later may differ from those turned in earlier. If this happens, new codes may have to be added later. If a researcher had decided to save time by starting coding as soon as the first questionnaires are turned in, such changes may require those doing the coding to go back and revise the codes assigned to earlier questionnaires. Given your small sample size, this should not present a serious problem.

Coding Procedures. Codes for open-ended questions should be created one question at a time. Several steps are typically involved in coding (Appendix 7A contains a coding form for you to use, or you may develop one of your own):

1. Randomly select at least fifty of the completed questionnaires. (In a large study, a larger number, say 150, would be desirable. The goal is to get a good representation of the responses among the total sample.)

2. Go through the responses to a single question, recording all that are relevant to the research objectives. In the case of OTHER, SPECIFY_____

questions, you should write down all additional items mentioned that were not included on the original listing. Write down as much as it takes to identify a unique response to open-ended questions such as advertising recall (e.g., "a man talking to a customer").

3.   Each unique response needs to be recorded only once on the coding form. However, in a separate column, you should keep track of the number of times the item is mentioned.

4.   After going through several questionnaires, a pattern should begin to emerge. Some responses will be mentioned often, while others will be mentioned by only one or two respondents. You will then have to decide which items to retain as a separate response and assign a code to each. Those items not assigned a unique code will be classified as "Other." In doing this, some things you should consider include:

   a.   It is important to try to keep the "Other" category fairly small, usually no more than 5 or, at the most, 10 percent of the total responses.

   b.   Responses that are mentioned only a few times will not be assigned unique codes unless they are of particular interest in the data analysis. These responses will be classified as "Other."

   c.   Assigning codes usually involves a trade-off between the above two considerations. The "Other" category should be small while at the same time a large number of codes should not be created that contain only a few responses.

5.   Once you have established the codes for all of the open-ended questions, you will go back through all of the questionnaires recording the codes for each response on the questionnaire. Usually, coding a single question on a complete pass through the entire set of questionnaires results in greater consistency. If several students are going to do the coding, each student should code an entire question. This also results in greater consistency in assigning codes.

DATA ENTRY

Data Analysis Programs.   You are ready to record the data in some form that may be processed by the computer once all of the questionnaires have been screened and all of the open-ended questions have been coded. Due to the small sizes of the data sets, some student teams are tempted to try to hand tabulate the data (by manually counting the responses). In the long run, this method will be very time-consuming and will probably cause you to do a much less sophisticated analysis than would otherwise result. If you are only interested in the simple frequencies of responses to each question, hand tabulation might be sufficient. However, suppose that you wanted a breakdown of male versus female respondents. This requires you to first separate the questionnaires into two groups (males and females) and then go back through and hand tabulate each group again. Attempting to perform several breakdowns this way requires several hand-tabulation passes through the entire set of questionnaires.

Another alternative that students have used is to try to tabulate data by using the database functions of standard spreadsheet or data base management programs. You will probably find that these programs are cumbersome to use for marketing research data. You will also be surprised at how easy it is to learn to use tabulation programs, such as SAS or SPSS.

Recording Data. You should go back and review the discussion of precoding in Chapter Four, even if you did not choose to preassign codes on the questionnaire, since much of that information will apply now.

Data is recorded on eighty-column records for input into most computer programs. You may have to use more than one eighty-column record for each respondent in order to record all the data if you have a long questionnaire. Once all your data is recorded, you will have a separate record (or set of records) for each respondent collected together in the form of a data set. It is this data set that will be subjected to computer analysis.

You must first establish a record format prior to entering any data. The entry of marketing research data usually uses a fixed-record format. This means each piece of data will be entered into the same column(s) for each respondent. Consider the following when making column assignments:

1. The first few columns of each data record should contain the interview number.

2. If you are using multiple records for each respondent, enter a number (e.g, 1, 2 or 3 if each respondent has three records) just after the interview number on each record.

3. The responses to screening questions are not normally entered as computer codes since the answers to all of these questions should be the same. For example, if one screening question were "Are you 18 years of age or older?", any negative responses would have resulted in a termination of the interview. Thus, all responses to this question on completed questionnaires would have to be "Yes."

4. Questions that have only one possible response will require only one column (or set of columns) for data recording. If there are more than nine responses to a question, you should use a set of two columns to contain the two-digit numbers used as codes (e.g., 01, 02, 11, 12, 13).

5.   You will need to leave a separate column (or set of columns) for each possible response if a question allows multiple responses. An example of a multiple response question is Question Two of Apex questionnaire, "Which dry cleaners have you seen advertised in the past month?" If two cleaners were mentioned, you could not record this in a single column. A separate column would be required for each response. Some specialized marketing research software packages do, in fact, allow "multipunched" data. However, this is cumbersome in the tabulation software you will be using.

Data Entry. There are two common ways of entering data if you are using a mainframe or a minicomputer for tabulation. You can enter information directly into the computer as a data set, or you can record the data on a personal computer using a word processor and then send the data set for storage on the mainframe.

The terminals of mainframe computers have either full-screen editors or line editors. A full-screen editor works essentially the same as a word processor, allowing easy editing of any character on the screen by simply moving the cursor to the desired position and inserting or deleting. Entering data using line editors, however, is cumbersome. You should consider entering the data using a word processor on a personal computer if your computer system uses a line editor.   Once your data set is completed on a word processor, it can be transferred to the mainframe through a modem and communications software. (Note, the data set from your word processor will probably have to be in ASCII format in order for it to be properly read and stored by the mainframe. If your word processor does not naturally store data in this form, it probably provides a utility for converting the file into ASCII format. If it doesn't you might consider some other type of word processing software.)

Normally, data entry is done directly from each questionnaire. If you have precoded the questionnaire, then the column assignments will allow you to check as you go along that you are entering each item of data in the proper column. This is very important because it is easy to forget to leave blank spaces when there is no data for the question. Forgeting to skip a space shifts all of the data on the record to the left, while entering an extra character shifts the data to the right. Since the computer reads all of the data for a certain question out of the same column, for instance column 32, if the data has been shifted in either direction, the data found in column 32 would actually belong to a different question. There is no way for the computer to compensate for this. It simply follows your instructions exactly (as computers always do), looking for all of the data for a single question in the column you have directed.

COMPUTER TABULATION

The two most common computer tabulation packages found on university mainframe or minicomputers are SAS (Statistical Analysis System) and SPSS (Statistical Package for the Social Sciences). Each of these programs has distinct advantages for performing various types of sophisticated analysis. However, for the purpose of data tabulation and simple analysis, the choice of a program is largely a matter of personal preference. Your instructor may suggest one or the other depending upon his or her previous experience.

Both SAS and SPSS have essentially the same capabilities. In the remainder of this chapter, we will use SAS commands to illustrate various procedures. An equivalent discussion is presented for SPSS in Appendix 7B. The discussion of SPSS is self-contained so that, if you choose to use it, you may skip directly to the appendix without reading the SAS discussion. If you have no previous experience with either program and your instructor has no preferences, you should read through both discussions and decide for yourself which appears more comfortable to use.

Your instructor will provide you with some essential information about your computer system along with account numbers and passwords. The first few lines of your computer program will be system commands that allow you to gain access to the system and to load the appropriate analysis package (in this case, SAS).

THE SAS PROGRAM

SAS Statements. There are many different types of statements in SAS. A few statements are required in every SAS program. Other statements are optional but are recommended since they will enhance the appearance of your final output. Only a few statements (plus your data set) are required to run the program and receive output.

A statement in SAS is always started with a keyword (we will use **BOLDFACE** Capital letters to refer to keywords) that is recognized by the program and causes some process to be performed on the remainder of the information on the line (and continuation lines, if used). SAS statements are always terminated with a semicolon. If there is no semicolon at the end of a line, the next line will be treated as a continuation of the previous line. In this sense, there is no limit to the length of a SAS statement. SAS statements may begin in any column. Typically, statements that are associated with the **DATA** statement and with other SAS procedures (**PROC**s) are indented a couple of spaces to set them off from other SAS procedures. However, this is not necessary.

Each time SAS reads a statement, it looks for the first word on the line (unless the line is a continuation of the previous line). SAS checks to determine if this word is a recognizable keyword. If SAS doesn't recognize the word, it will issue an error message.

DATA Statement. The data statement is used to provide a name for your SAS data set. The form of the data statement is:

```
DATA Cleaners;
```

The word following the word **DATA** is a name you provide and it must start with an alphabetic character. It may be up to eight characters long. It is possible to create and

TABLE 7.1
SAMPLE SAS PROGRAM TO ACCOMPANY APEX QUESTIONNAIRE

```
DATA CLEANERS;
INPUT     A1 4 A2 5 A3 6 A4 7 A5 8 A6 9 A7 10 A8 11 A9 12-13
          A10 14-15 A11 16 A12 17 A13 18 A14 19 A15 20 A16 21
          A17 22 A18 23 A19 24 A20 25 A21 26 A22 27 A23 28 A24 29
          A25 30 A26 31 A27 32 A28 33 A29 34 A30 35 A31 36 A32 37
          A33 38 A34 39 A35 40 A36 41 A37 42 A38 43 A39 44 A40 45
          A41 46 A42 47;
LABEL
      A1='RECALL OF APEX'
      A2='RECALL OF COMET'
      A3='RECALL OF ONE HOUR'
      A4='RECALL OF OTHER CLEANERS'
      A5='SEEN ADS FOR APEX?'
      A6='SEEN ADS FOR COMET?'
      A7='SEEN ADS FOR ONE HOUR?'
      A8='SEEN ADS FOR OTHER COMPANIES?'
      A9='FIRST THING RECALLED ABOUT APEX ADS'
      A10='SECOND THING RECALLED ABOUT APEX ADS'
      A11='MONTHLY SPENDING, DRY CLEANING'
      A12='MONTHLY SPENDING, LAUNDRY'
      A13='DO YOU EVER USE COUPONS?'
      A14='TYPE COUPON MOST PREFERRED'
      A15='CLEANERS USED MOST OFTEN'
      A16='DISTANCE FROM APEX'
      A17='RATING-SERVICE-APEX'
      A18='RATING-SPECIALS-APEX'
      A19='RATING-PRICES-APEX'
      A20='RATING-LOCATION-APEX'
      A21='RATING-HOURS-APEX'
      A22='RATING-SERVICE-COMET'
      A23='RATING-SPECIALS-COMET'
      A24='RATING-PRICES-COMET'
      A25='RATING-LOCATION-COMET'
      A26='RATING-HOURS-COMET'
      A27='RATING-SERVICE-ONE HOUR'
      A28='RATING-SPECIALS-ONE HOUR'
      A29='RATING-PRICES-ONE HOUR'
      A30='RATING-LOCATION-ONE HOUR'
      A31='RATING-HOURS-ONE HOUR'
      A32='IMPORTANCE-SERVICE'
      A33='IMPORTANCE-SPECIALS'
      A34='IMPORTANCE-PRICES'
      A35='IMPORTANCE-LOCATION'
      A36='IMPORTANCE-HOURS'
      A37='SEX OF RESPONDENT'
      A38='AGE OF RESPONDENT'
      A39='MARITAL STATUS'
      A40='SIZE OF HOUSEHOLD'
```

```
            A41='OCCUPATION'
            A42='INCOME'
            A11X='DRY CLEANING SPENDING - RESCALED'
            A12X='LAUNDRY SPENDING - RESCALED'
            SPENDTOT='TOTAL SPENDING - DC + LAUNDRY'
            A16X='DISTANCE FROM APEX - RESCALED'
            MOST='CLEANERS USED MOST OFTEN'
            DIST='DUMMY FOR DISTANCE FROM APEX'
            A38X='RESPONDENT AGE - RESCALED'
            A42X='RESPONDENT INCOME - RESCALED';
            IF (A1=.)THEN A1=3; IF (A2=.)THEN A2=3;
            IF(A3=.)THEN A3=3; IF(A4=.)THEN A4=3;
            IF (A5=.)THEN A5=2; IF (A6=.)THEN A6=2;
            IF (A7=.)THEN A7=2; IF (A8=.)THEN A7=2;
            IF(A11=1)THEN A11X=5; IF(A11=2)THEN A11X=15.5;
            IF(A11=3)THEN A11X=28;IF(A11=4)THEN A11X=42.5;
            IF(A11=5)THEN A11X=62.5;IF(A11=6)THEN A11X=82.5;
            IF(A11=7)THEN A11X=125;
            IF(A12=1)THEN A12X=5; IF(A12=2)THEN A12X=15.5;
            IF(A12=3)THEN A12X=28;IF(A12=4)THEN A12X=42.5;
            IF(A12=5)THEN A12X=62.5;IF(A12=6)THEN A12X=82.5;
            IF(A12=7)THEN A12X=125;
            SPENDTOT=A11X + A12X ;
            IF(A16=1)THEN A16X=.5; IF(A16=2)THEN A16X= 1.5;
            IF(A16=3)THEN A16X=2.5; IF (A16=4)THEN A16X=4;
            IF(A16=5)THEN A16X = 6;
            IF(A15 EQ 1) THEN MOST = 1;
            IF(A15 EQ 2 OR A15 EQ 3 OR A15 EQ 4) THEN MOST = 2;
            IF(A16=1 OR A16 = 2)THEN DIST=1;
            IF(A16=3 OR A16=4 OR A16=5)THEN DIST = 2;
            IF(A38=1)THEN A38X=19; IF(A38=2)THEN A38X=23;
            IF(A38=3)THEN A38X=25.5;  IF(A38=4)THEN A38X=42.5;
            IF(A38=5)THEN A38X=59.5; IF (A38=6)THEN A38X=80;
            IF(A42=1)THEN A42X=7500; IF(A42=2)THEN A42X=20000;
            IF(A42=3)THEN A42X=32500; IF(A42=4)THEN A42X=50000;
            IF(A42=5)THEN A42X=80000; IF(A42=6)THEN A42X=150000;
CARDS;
    (Data Set Goes Here)
;
DATA LABELSET;
        PROC FORMAT;
            VALUE   RCLFMT 1='UNAIDED' 2='AIDED' 3='UNAWARE';
            VALUE   ADFMT 1='YES' 2='NO' .='REFUSED';
            VALUE   ITEMFMT 1='HIGH QUALITY' 2='EXTRA CARE'
                    3='ALL COUPONS' 4='SPECIALS' 5='FRIENDLY SERVICE'
                    6='VALUE-Q VS PRICE' 7='SPECIALTY ITEMS';
            VALUE   SPENDFMT 1='LESS TH $10' 2='$11-$20' 3='$21-$35'
                    4='$35-$50'  5='$50-$75' 6='$75-$100'
                    7='MORE TH $100' .='REFUSED';
            VALUE   YESNOFMT 1='YES' 2='NO' .='REFUSED';
            VALUE   CPNFMT 1='PRICE OFF' 2='SUITS'
                    3='SLACKS' 4='SHIRTS & BLS' .='REFUSED OR DK';
```

```
          VALUE    MOSTFMT 1='APEX' 2='COMET' 3='ONE HOUR'
                   6='OTHER' .='REFUSED';
          VALUE    DISTFMT 1='LESS TH 1 MILE' 2='1 TO < 2 MI'
                   3='2 TO < 3 MI' 4='3 TO < 5  MI' 5='5 MILES OR >'
                   .='REFUSED';
          VALUE    RATEFMT 1='EXCELLENT' 2='GOOD' 3='FAIR'
                   4='POOR'.='REFUSED OR DK';
          VALUE    IMPFMT 1='EXTREMELY' 2='VERY' 3='SOMEWHAT'
                   4='NOT IMP' .='REFUSED OR DK';
          VALUE    SEXFMT 1='MALE' 2='FEMALE';
          VALUE    MSTATFMT 1='SINGLE' 2='MARRIED' 3='SEP,DIV, WIDOW'
                   .='REFUSED';
          VALUE    AGEFMT 1='UNDER 21' 2='21 TO 25' 3='26 TO 35'
                   4='36 TO 49' 5='50 TO 69' 6='70 OR OLDER'
                   .='REFUSED OR DK';
          VALUE    INCFMT 1='$15K OR LESS' 2='$15K TO $25 K'
                   3='$25K TO $40K' 4='40K TO $60K'
                   5='$60K TO $100K' 6='OVER $100 K'
                   .='REFUSED OR DK';
          VALUE NEWDIST 1='< 2 MILES' 2='2 OR MORE MILES';
          VALUE NEWMOST 1='APEX' 2='OTHER';
TITLE 'APEX DRY CLEANING STUDY - TEAM THREE - FALL 1993';
PROC FREQ DATA=CLEANERS;
     TITLE2 'SAS FREQUENCY DISTRIBUTIONS';
     FORMAT A1--A4 RCLFMT. A5--A8 ADFMT. A9--A10 ITEMFMT.
      A11 A12 SPENDFMT. A13 YESNOFMT. A14 CPNFMT. A15 MOSTFMT.
      A16 DISTFMT. A17--A31 RATEFMT. A32--A36 IMPFMT.
      A37 SEXFMT. A38 AGEFMT. A39 MSTATFMT. A42 INCFMT. MOST
      NEWMOST. DIST NEWDIST.;
PROC MEANS DATA=CLEANERS;
     VAR A16X;
PROC FREQ DATA=CLEANERS;
     TITLE2 'SAS CROSS-TABULATIONS';
        FORMAT A15 MOSTFMT. A16 DISTFMT.;
        TABLES A16*A15/CHISQ;
PROC FREQ DATA=CLEANERS;
     TITLE2 'SAS CROSS-TABULATIONS';
        FORMAT A15 MOSTFMT. A16 DISTFMT.;
        TABLES A16*A15/CHISQ NOPERCENT NOCOL;
PROC MEANS DATA=CLEANERS;
     VAR A16X;
PROC SORT DATA = CLEANERS;
     BY A15;
PROC MEANS DATA=CLEANERS;
     BY A15;
     VAR A16X;
PROC FREQ DATA=CLEANERS;
     FORMAT MOST NEWMOST. DIST NEWDIST.;
     TABLES DIST*MOST/CHISQ NOPERCENT NOCOL;
PROC MEANS DATA=CLEANERS;
     VAR A16X;
PROC SORT DATA=CLEANERS;
```

```
     BY MOST;
PROC MEANS DATA=CLEANERS;
     BY MOST;
     VAR A16X;
;
```

work with several data sets at the same time during a SAS run. Some procedures that will be discussed later may require you to specify the name of the data set on which the procedure will be performed.

INPUT Statement. The line after the **DATA** statement is the **INPUT** statement This statement specifies the format of each line of data that the computer is to read. The sample program in Table 7.1 contains a typical data statement. Here is another:

```
INPUT     A1 5 A2 6 A3 7 A4 8 A5 9 A6 10 A7 11 A8 12 A9 13
          A10 14 A11 15-16 A12 17-18 A13 19 A14 20
          A15 21-22  A16 23-24 A17 25-26 A18 27 A19 28 A20 29
          A21 30 A22 31 A23 32 A24 33 A25 34 A26 35 A27 36
          A28 37 A29 38 A30 39 A31 40 A32 41-42 A33 43-44
          A34 45-46 A35 47-48 A36 49 A37 50  #2 A38 5 A39 6
          A40 7 A41 8 A42 9 A43 10 A44 11 A45 12;
```

The **INPUT** specification above indicates that each subject will have two records (lines of data). Just after the word **INPUT** (followed by one or more blank spaces), you list the format by which SAS will read the first record for each subject. When subjects have multiple records, it is necessary to indicate where the record format for subsequent lines begins. The characters #2 (on the sixth line of the above **INPUT** statement) appear after the entire format for the first line of data and cause the program to interpret the remainder of the format as applying to the second data record for each subject.

Each question in the questionnaire represents one or more pieces of information (depending upon whether it is a single-response or multiple-response question). Each piece of information is identified within the program by a variable name. Variable names can be short (even a single letter is sufficient) or up to eight characters long and may contain letters and numbers. The variable names must begin with an alphabetic character. Numbers have been used to identify the variable names in this example (i.e. A1 through A42). If you decide to not provide labels for your questions and answers (to be discussed shortly) you may choose to use more descriptive names for your variables (e.g. RCLAPEX for recall of Apex, ADVAPEX for advertising for APEX).

Each variable name is followed by the column number(s) from which the data is to be read. In the above example, the program will not read any data out of columns 1 through 4. In the Apex questionnaire, these columns contain the interview ID number and the record ID. The numbers in these columns merely serve to identify the interview number and the line of the set of multiple records. Later, if you need to locate a data record in the file, this information may be useful.   Variables A1 through A10 will be read out of the next ten columns (5 through 14). Variable A11 is a two-digit variable read from columns 15 and 16, and so on.

The #2 indicates the beginning of the format for the second line of data. On the second line of data for each subject, the first four columns (containing the interview and record

ID's) are again skipped and variable A38 is read out of column 5 of the second data record for each subject, A39 out of column 6, and so on.

Note also in our example that the **INPUT** statement is too long to fit on a single line. Thus, only the last line ends with a semicolon and the program will treat all seven lines as continuations of the first line. In addition, for the sake of appearance and readability, only the word **INPUT** starts in column 1 and the remainder of the lines have been indented. Until the program encounters a semicolon, blanks either within the line or at the end of the line are ignored. It is only necessary that information items (keywords, variable names etc.) are separated by one or more blank spaces.

CARDS Statement. It would be possible to run our example program with only two additional SAS statements (other than our data set):

```
CARDS;
    (Data set)
;
```

The **CARDS** statement tells the program that the lines that follow are not SAS statements but are actual lines of data (from the data set you created from the questionnaires). Insert a line containing a single semicolon after all the data lines to tell the program to stop reading data and to resume processing SAS statements. You may include as many lines of data as you wish, from a small number (for instance, five lines to run a test of the program) to literally hundreds of thousands. In fact, you can run the program with no data at all to get an error check of all the SAS statements.

Following the data set and the terminating semicolon, you place additional statements that request SAS to perform various procedures on your data, such as tabulations and cross-tabulations. We will discuss these procedures in Chapter Eight.

TITLE Statement. The **TITLE** statement is optional but is suggested because it will print the name of your project at the top of every page of computer output.

```
TITLE 'APEX DRY CLEANING STUDY - TEAM THREE - FALL 1993';
```

Notice that after the keyword **TITLE**, there is a blank space. After this space, you may type any title you wish (enclosed in single or double quotation marks). Up to ten titles may be printed on each page of SAS output. Adding a number after the word **TITLE** indicates the output line on which the title will appear (a title with no number is equivalent to **TITLE1**.) These titles will be centered on the page and will be presented, one above the other. Titles may be up to 132 characters in length.

```
TITLE 'APEX DRY CLEANING STUDY - TEAM THREE - FALL 1993';
TITLE2 'SAS FREQUENCY DISTRIBUTIONS';
```

The titles above would appear, centered, on lines 1 and 2 of each page of output. In our example SAS program (Table 7.1), we have placed a title statement just after the end of the data set. Within the SAS **PROC** itself we may place additional **TITLE** statements to identify each separate run of the program.

Labeling Questions. You might also want to include **LABEL** and **FORMAT** statements in your program. These two optional commands tell the program to print the text of the questions and answers on the printed output when SAS procedures are performed. This labeling can be very valuable when the time comes to read and interpret your printouts. Without it, the printout will only contain variable names and the numerical codes which identify the responses. You will have to constantly refer to your questionnaire to determine which question was associated with the variable and which answers are associated with the coded responses. This is not only inconvenient but is also a potential source of error in transposition and interpretation.

LABELS correspond to the text of the questions, while **FORMAT** corresponds to the text of the answers. For example:

```
LABEL        A1='RECALL OF APEX'
             A2='RECALL OF COMET'
             A3='RECALL OF ONE HOUR'
             A4='RECALL OF OTHER CLEANERS'
                   (Additional labels for variables)
             A42='INCOME';
```

The above statement will cause the program to associate labels with each of the variables. These labels are limited to forty characters in length, so you may have to use some creativity in abbreviating the text of the question. You may have several **LABELS** statements if you desire. However, a single **LABELS** statement may be continued for as many lines as necessary to provide all your value labels (as in the example above). Don't forget to enclose each label in single quote marks and to terminate the last line, and only the last line, with a semicolon. The label statement may be placed just after the **INPUT** statement and before the **CARDS** statement

Labeling Responses. It is also possible to associate labels with the answers to each question. In order to do this, it is first necessary to create response formats:

```
DATA LABELSET;
PROC FORMAT;
  VALUE      RCLFMT 1='UNAIDED' 2='AIDED';
  VALUE      ADFMT 1='SEEN ADS';
  VALUE      SPENDFMT 1='LESS TH $10' 2='$11-$20 3='$21-$35'
             4='$35-$50'  5='$50-$75' 6='$75-$100'
             7='MORE TH $100';
  VALUE      RATEFMT 1='EXCELLENT' 2='GOOD' 3='FAIR' 4='POOR';
```

The set of lines above creates formats that will be used to identify the responses to each question. It is best to put the **PROC FORMAT** statement and its associated **VALUE** statements after the data set but before any SAS procedures you intend to request on a particular SAS run. **PROC FORMAT** is a SAS procedure which specifies and prepares a separate data set for saving your output formats. These formats may be used later when requesting output from other SAS **PROC** statement. Note that we begin specifying formats with a **DATA** statement and we have requested SAS to store these formats in a data set called LABELSET (you could choose any name you choose for the name of the data set to store your formats). Later these formats will be retrieved from LABELSET as needed to provide labeling for our output.

The text of the answers to the questions is associated with variable names which you will assign. These variable names must be different from the names of the variables you used on the **INPUT** statement. In our example we have used the variable names RCLFMT (for brand recall questions), ADFMT (for advertising recall) and SPENDFMT (for the format for laundry and dry cleaning spending). If you have many questions that all have the same set of responses (e.g a number of YES/NO or scaled questions), you only have to specify a format once in order to use it with any of them. After creating the format, you can refer to it as often as necessary to request the labeling to be associated with any table of output.

After the **PROC FORMAT** statement, you will have **VALUE** statements, one for each set of responses. After the word **VALUE,** place the variable name you have chosen to associate with the format. Next, each answer code is listed followed by an equal sign and the text of the response associated with the code, enclosed in single quotation marks. After providing this information for a format, a semicolon is entered and another set of labels may be specified in the same fashion. The text of the answer cannot exceed sixteen characters in length, so careful abbreviation may be required (e.g., Refused or Don't Know = RFSD OR DK). The variables, codes, and the text of the responses may be continued onto as many lines as necessary for each value statement. After terminating the **VALUE** statement with a semicolon, you may specify another. In Chapter Eight, when we discuss SAS analysis procedures, we will show you how to use these formats when requesting output.

Variable Transformations. When the SAS program runs, it reads your input data and stores it in the computer's memory. When you request procedures (e.g., tabulations) to be performed, it will operate on the stored data values. Initially, the data that is stored is exactly the same as the data in the lines of your input data set. However, it is possible to transform this data or to add new variables to the data set. These new variables are usually combinations of the original variables or are related to them in some way.

An important type of variable transformation is the SAS expression. Expressions are sequences of operators and operands that perform a set of instructions to produce a desired result. One use for these expressions is to allow you to create new variables based upon the values in the stored data set. These are new variables that were not specified on the **INPUT** statement. However, once they are created, they may be used just as any other variables.

Suppose we had two variables, A11X, "How much do you spend on dry cleaning per month?" and A12X, "How much do you spend on laundry per month?" Perhaps it would be useful to have an additional variable that would provide the total amount spent. The following expression could be used to create such a variable:

```
SPENDTOT= A11X + A12X;
```

We have created a new variable that we have given the variable name SPENDTOT and is the sum of the two variables A11X and A12X. In the expression, the original variables, A11X and A12X, are unaffected by this transformation. However, the new variable, SPENDTOT, is available to be used just as we use any of the variables read in on the original **INPUT** statement.

The most commonly used expressions are arithmetic statements. This is because most operations performed on the data are numerical operations. Expressions allow the use of all of the common arithmetical operations such as plus, minus, asterisk, and slash to indicate addition, subtraction, multiplication and division. Expressions also allow a wide variety of more complex mathematical functions, such as logarithms and exponentiation (see the SAS manual for a complete discussion).

Another very useful transformation is the **IF** statement. This statement can be used in a variety of ways. It is expressed in the form:

```
IF condition THEN expression;
```

where "condition" is a combination of logical operators and "expression" is any valid SAS expression as described earlier. If the condition is evaluated as "true," then the expression is executed, if "false" the expression is ignored. Operators that may be used in the "condition" portion of the statement may be either symbols or abbreviations:

SYMBOL	ABBREVIATION	MEANING
<	LT	Less than
< =	LE	Less than or equal to
>	GT	Greater than
> =	GE	Greater than or equal to
=	EQ	Equal to
< >	NE	Not equal to

One convenient use for the **IF** statement is to provide values for variables that are part of skip patterns. Suppose that we had the following two questions:

6.   **Do you ever use dry cleaning coupons?**

(18)

YES **1**
NO (SKIP TO QUESTION 8) **2**
REFUSED OR DON'T KNOW (SKIP TO QUESTION 8) **8**

7.   **When you use coupons, what one type do you most prefer. Would it be (READ LIST BELOW)?**

(19)

Price off, such as $ 1 off on a $ 10 order **1**
Special prices on suits **2**
Special prices on slacks **3**
Special prices on laundered shirts and blouses **4**
REFUSED OR DON'T KNOW **8**

If the interviewers follow the instructions exactly, a NO or REFUSED response on Question Six would cause a skip to Question Eight. Thus, there would be no reason to enter a coded response to Question Seven. Perhaps, later, we might decide that we would like the not applicable responses identified with a special code, say code 9. Of course, this Code 9 could be recorded in the editing process and entered during the data entry process. However, the SAS **IF** statement provides a convenient way to ensure the proper coding of Question Seven.

```
IF (A13 NE 1) THEN A14 = 9;
```

Note that the **IF** statement has two parts, a condition (A13 NE 1) and an expression (A14 = 9). If the condition is true (that is A13 has not been coded a 1), the result is executed. If the condition is false (A13 received a code of 1), then the result is ignored and not executed.

Note also that the result following the condition is not a logical operator but rather an arithmetic expression. In essence, the result portion of the **IF** statement is equivalent to other SAS expressions that perform arithmetic operations. However, the computation is performed only if the conditional is true.

Another important use of the **IF** statement is to change the values that are stored in computer memory. For instance, suppose that in our question "Which dry cleaners do you use most often?" we had two dry cleaners (M Cleaners-Code 4, and Vogue-Code 5) as well as an "Other" category (Code 6). Suppose that there were very few Code 4 and 5 responses and we wanted to assign them to the "Other" category to simplify our output and analysis. The following **IF** statements could be used:

```
IF (A15 EQ 4) THEN A15 = 6;
IF (A15 EQ 5) THEN A15 = 6;
```

A simpler form of the above statement would be:

```
IF (A15 EQ 4 OR A15 EQ 5) THEN A15 = 6;
```

Another way that the **IF** statement is often used is to create new variables from the original variables that were entered as a part of the data set. This may be done to create pseudo-interval variables which will have some of the qualities of true interval-scaled variables. You may recall from your textbook that the arithmetic mean may only properly be calculated from interval data. Nevertheless, the data you enter into your data set is usually nominal or ordinal. The original codes and the responses for variable A16 ("How far is Apex from your home?") are presented below:

Code	Response
1	Less than one mile
2	One to less than two miles
3	Two to less than three miles
4	Three to less than five miles
5	Five miles or more

If you request that the program calculate the mean for variable A16, it would calculate the mean of the **codes**. These codes bear a rough relationship to the distance the respondent lives from the store. However, an average value of, for instance, 2.63 would be difficult to interpret. The codes can be transformed into a better representation of distance.

Suppose that you were able to know the exact distance from the store for all those who responded "One mile or less." What do you suppose would be the average distance for these respondents? Most people would probably guess that the average distance is somewhere around one-half mile. For those in the second category, a good estimate would be 1.5 miles. You would probably use 2.5 miles for those in the third category. The top category presents a bit of a problem since it has no upper bound. But if you assume that people are not likely to travel great distances to a dry cleaning establishment, you might estimate that the average distance within this highest group is 6.0 miles.

You can use the following **IF** statements to create a new variable (we will call it A16X) with these transformed values:

```
IF    (A16 EQ 1) THEN A16X = .5;
IF    (A16 EQ 2) THEN A16X = 1.5;
IF    (A16 EQ 3) THEN A16X = 2.5;
IF    (A16 EQ 4) THEN A16X = 4.0;
IF    (A16 EQ 5) THEN A16X = 6.0;
```

When the above statements are encountered, the program will go through all the stored values for variable A16 in the internal data set, test them, and assign the appropriate value to variable A16X according to which **IF** statement is true. Note that in our example program

(Table 7.1) we have added a **LABEL** to variable A16X so that it may be easily identified when we use it later in a SAS procedure.

Missing Values. In Chapter Eight, we will discuss some of the common types of SAS procedures that you will use in your data analysis. Each of these procedures will treat "missing values" differently than "nonmissing" values. We mentioned missing values in Chapter Five in our discussion of questionnaire design. There are several ways of assigning values as missing. When SAS reads the data set, any column that is left blank or into which is entered a single period (.) will automatically be treated as a missing value.

Sometimes you will want to designate specific responses, such as "REFUSED" or "NOT APPLICABLE" as missing values. Consider the following question:

8.   **Which dry cleaners do you use most often?**

                                                                                          (20)
    APEX 1
    COMET 2
    ONE HOUR 3
    OTHER SPECIFY_____   .... ____
    REFUSED OR DON'T KNOW 8

In the above example, the computer would treat the code 8s in the same way as any other values. However, if we want percentages based upon the percent of meaningful responses, we could use the following SAS statement to change the code 8s to missing values.

```
IF (A15 = 8) THEN A15 =.;
```

All code 8s for variable A15 will be changed to the value (.) and will be treated the same as if the original data set contained a blank column or a column in which the period was specified.

As we mentioned earlier, when a blank column is read, it will automatically be treated as a missing value. Sometimes we will want to transform these missing values to new values that will not be treated as missing, for example, when a blank response should be treated as a "NO." The following statements would accomplish this for variable A5:

```
IF (A5=.)THEN A5=2; IF (A6=.)THEN A6=2;
IF (A7=.)THEN A7=2; IF (A8=.)THEN A8=2;
```

After executing this statement, the data set, would contain only the values "1" and "2" for the variables A5 through A8.

Order of Command Lines. Some SAS statements may be placed anywhere in the program while others must be placed in a specific order. You should consult the SAS manual for a discussion of the various placements of SAS procedures. Below, is a suggested ordering of

SAS procedures. It is not the only way to set up a SAS job. However, as a general rule, it should allow you to avoid errors.

```
System Control Lines
DATA;
INPUT;
LABEL;
IF statements and SAS expressions;
CARDS;
     (data set)
;
TITLE;
DATA;
PROC FORMAT;
SAS PROCEDURES;
;
```

SAS Error Messages. There are a host of errors that might be made in an SAS program, and, at least on the first few tests of your program, you are almost certain to see some of them. Some of the more common errors include:

1.   Error in system statements. This is usually indicated when you do not get back anything that resembles an SAS program. System statements provide instructions to your computer system. They are not a part of the SAS procedures. Usually, they are placed before any part of your SAS program. Usually, when a system error is encountered, an immediate error message is issued and none of the remainder of the program is processed. Since no SAS statements are processed, no SAS output is produced.

2.   Errors on the **INPUT** statement. Even if the **INPUT** statement does not cause an error, you should carefully check your data format to ensure that the data will be read out of the proper columns.

3.   Unrecognized keywords. All keywords (e.g., **TITLE, DATA, INPUT,** and **LABEL**) must be spelled correctly to be recognized by the program. The first word of a SAS statement must be a recognizable keyword.

4.   Unknown variable. This occurs when a variable name is encountered that has not been previously created by the **INPUT** statement or a SAS expression.

5.   Errors in punctuation. On the **LABEL** statement, the label itself is enclosed in single quotation marks. It is also easy to forget to enter the terminating semicolon. Punctuation is especially important on the **PROC FORMAT** statement. The actual codes are not enclosed in quotation marks but each label must begin and end with the single quotation mark.

6.   Missing **CARDS** statement or missing semicolon to terminate the data set. The **CARDS** statement tells the program to begin reading data from your data set. If it were left off, the program would attempt to read lines of the data set as program statements. This would cause an error since they do not begin with keywords. On the other hand, if the semicolon at the end of the data set were not included, program statements would be treated as though they were part of the data set. Usually this causes a series of errors when the alphabetic characters of the statement are not recognized as numbers.

7.   Missing semicolon at the end of a SAS statement. This very common error will cause a line of data to be read as a continuation of a previous line. It may cause the generation of a number of different, and often confusing, SAS error messages, all associated with this one small error.

APPENDIX 7A
CODING SHEET FOR OPEN ENDED QUESTIONS

QUESTION # _____   VARIABLE ID _____   VARIABLE LABEL(S)_____

CODE FIRST 1 2 3 ITEM(S)   ITEM   RECORD   COLUMN(S)
                 MENTIONED   FIRST   ____   ____ ____
                             SECOND   ____   ____ ____
                             THIRD   ____   ____ ____

CODE	RESPONSE DESCRIPTION
01	
02	
03	
04	
05	
06	
07	
11	
12	
13	
14	
15	
16	
17	
18	
19	
21	
22	
23	
08 OR 88	REFUSED OR DON'T KNOW
09 OR 99	NOT APPLICABLE

Codes 10 and 20 are not used to minimize data entry errors.
Codes 08, 88, 09 and 99 are reserved for REFUSED and NOT APPLICABLE responses.

117

CODING SHEET FOR OPEN ENDED QUESTIONS

QUESTION # _____   VARIABLE ID _____   VARIABLE LABEL(S)_____

CODE FIRST 1 2 3 ITEM(S)   <u>ITEM</u>   <u>RECORD</u>   <u>COLUMN(S)</u>
                 MENTIONED   FIRST
                                SECOND   _____   _____ _____
                                THIRD   _____   _____ _____

CODE	RESPONSE DESCRIPTION
01	
02	
03	
04	
05	
06	
07	
11	
12	
13	
14	
15	
16	
17	
18	
19	
21	
22	
23	
24	
08 OR 88	REFUSED OR DON'T KNOW
09 OR 99	NOT APPLICABLE

Codes 10 and 20 are not used to minimize data entry errors.
Codes 08, 88, 09 and 99 are reserved for REFUSED and NOT APPLICABLE responses.

CODING SHEET FOR OPEN ENDED QUESTIONS

QUESTION # ____   VARIABLE ID ____   VARIABLE LABEL(S)_____

CODE FIRST 1 2 3	ITEM(S) MENTIONED	ITEM	RECORD	COLUMN(S)
		FIRST	___	___ ___
		SECOND	___	___ ___
		THIRD	___	___ ___

CODE	RESPONSE DESCRIPTION
01	
02	
03	
04	
05	
06	
07	
11	
12	
13	
14	
15	
16	
17	
18	
19	
21	
22	
23	
24	
08 OR 88	REFUSED OR DON'T KNOW
09 OR 99	NOT APPLICABLE

Codes 10 and 20 are not used to minimize data entry errors.
Codes 08, 88, 09 and 99 are reserved for REFUSED and NOT APPLICABLE responses.

CODING SHEET FOR OPEN ENDED QUESTIONS

QUESTION # _____   VARIABLE ID _____   VARIABLE LABEL(S)_____

CODE FIRST 1 2 3   ITEM(S)   ITEM   RECORD   COLUMN(S)
                      MENTIONED   FIRST   _____   _____ _____
                                   SECOND   _____   _____ _____
                                   THIRD   _____   _____ _____

CODE	RESPONSE DESCRIPTION
01	
02	
03	
04	
05	
06	
07	
11	
12	
13	
14	
15	
16	
17	
18	
19	
21	
22	
23	
24	
08 OR 88	REFUSED OR DON'T KNOW
09 OR 99	NOT APPLICABLE

Codes 10 and 20 are not used to minimize data entry errors.
Codes 08, 88, 09 and 99 are reserved for REFUSED and NOT APPLICABLE responses.

APPENDIX 7B
SPSS PROGRAMMING

This appendix substantially duplicates the discussion presented in Chapter Seven. However, it will apply entirely to SPSS programming.

SPSS Statements. A statement in SPSS is always started with a keyword (we will use **BOLDFACE** CAPITALS for keywords). Keywords are recognized by the program and cause some process to be performed on the remainder of the information on the line (and continuation lines, if used). Each time SPSS reads a line of the program, it looks in the first column of the line. If the first column on the line is left blank, SPSS assumes that the line is a continuation of a previous line. If not a program line and if the first column is not blank, SPSS checks to see if the line was started with a keyword. If it does not find a keyword, it will issue an error message.

Title Statement. Usually the first program line you will enter (after the system lines used to access the SPSS program) is the **TITLE** line. This is an optional statement but is suggested because it will print the name of your project at the top of every page of output.

```
TITLE APEX DRY CLEANING STUDY
```

Notice that after the keyword **TITLE** there is a blank space. After this space, you may use the remainder of the line to type any title you wish. You may have only one **TITLE** line.

INPUT Statement. The line after the **TITLE** statement will usually be the **DATA LIST** statement. This statement specifies the format of each line of data that the computer is to read. The sample program in Table 7B.1 contains a typical data statement. Here is another:

```
DATA LIST RECORDS = 2/1 A1 TO A10 5-14 A11 15-16 A12 TO A15
        17-20 A16 A17 21-24 A18 TO A20 26-28 /2 A21 to A40 5-24
```

The RECORDS=2/1 specification indicates that each subject will have two records. The "2" indicates that there are two records for each subject. The "1" indicates that what follows is the format for the first line of data for each subject. Just after the 2/1 characters (followed by one or more blank spaces), you list the format by which SPSS will read the first record for each subject. When subjects have multiple records, it is necessary to indicate where the record format for subsequent lines begins. The characters /2 (on the second line of the above **DATA LIST** statement) appear after the entire format for the first line of data and cause the program to interpret the remainder of the format as applying to the second data record for each subject.

TABLE 7B.1
SAMPLE SPSS PROGRAM TO ACCOMPANY APEX QUESTIONNAIRE

```
UNNUMBERED
TITLE 'APEX DRY CLEANING STUDY - TEAM THREE '
DATA LIST RECORDS = 1/1 A1 TO A8 4-11 A9 12-13
   A10 14-15 A11 TO A42 16-47
RECODE A1 TO A4 (SYSMIS=8)
RECODE A5 TO A8 (SYSMIS=8)
RECODE A5 TO A8 (0=2)
RECODE A9 A10 (SYSMIS=88)
RECODE A11 TO A42 (SYSMIS=8)
IF (A5 NE 1) A9 =99
IF (A5 NE 1) A10 =99
IF (A13 NE 1)A14=9
IF (A11 EQ  1) A11X=5
IF (A11 EQ  2) A11X=15.5
IF (A11 EQ 3) A11X=28
IF (A11 EQ 4) A11X=42.5
IF (A11 EQ 5) A11X=62.5
IF (A11 EQ 6) A11X=82.5
IF (A11 EQ 7) A11X=125
IF (A12 EQ 1) A12X=5
IF (A12 EQ 2)A12X=15.5
IF (A12 EQ 3) A12X=28
IF (A12 EQ 4) A12X=42.5
IF (A12 EQ 5) A12X=62.5
IF (A12 EQ 6) A12X=82.5
IF (A12 EQ 7) A12X=125
COMPUTE SPENDTOT=A11X + A12X
IF (A16 EQ 1) A16X=.5
IF (A16 EQ 2) A16X= 1.5
IF (A16 EQ 3) A16X=2.5
IF (A16 EQ 4) A16X=4
IF (A16 EQ 5) A16X = 6
IF (A15 EQ 1) MOST= 1
IF (A15 EQ 2 OR A15 EQ 3 OR A15 EQ 4) MOST = 2
IF (A16 EQ 1 OR A16 EQ 2) DIST=1
IF (A16 EQ 3 OR A16 EQ 4 OR A16 EQ 5) DIST = 2
IF (A38 EQ 1) A38X=19
IF (A38 EQ 2) A38X=23
IF (A38 EQ 3) A38X=25.5
IF (A38 EQ 4) A38X=42.5
IF (A38 EQ 5) A38X=59.5
IF (A38 EQ 6) A38X=80
IF (A42 EQ 1) A42X=7500
IF (A42 EQ 2) A42X=20000
IF (A42 EQ 3) A42X=32500
IF (A42 EQ 4) A42X=50000
IF (A42 EQ 5) A42X=80000
```

```
IF (A42 EQ 6) A42X=150000
VARIABLE LABELS
  A1  'RECALL OF APEX'
  A2  'RECALL OF COMET'
  A3  'RECALL OF ONE HOUR'
  A4  'RECALL OF OTHERS'
  A5  'SEEN ADS FOR APEX?'
  A6  'SEEN ADS FOR COMET?'
  A7  'SEEN ADS FOR ONE HOUR?'
  A8  'OTHER COMPANIES SEEN ADS FOR?'
  A9  'FIRST THING RECALLED ABOUT APEX ADS'
  A10 'SECOND THING RECALLED ABOUT APEX ADS'
  A11 'MONTHLY SPENDING, DRY CLEANING'
  A12 'MONTHLY SPENDING, LAUNDRY'
  A13 'DO YOU EVER USE COUPONS?'
  A14 'TYPE COUPON MOST PREFERRED'
  A15 'CLEANERS USED MOST OFTEN'
  A16 'DISTANCE FROM APEX'
  A17 'RATING-SERVICE-APEX'
  A18 'RATING-SPECIALS-APEX'
  A19 'RATING-PRICES-APEX'
  A20 'RATING-LOCATION-APEX'
  A21 'RATING-HOURS-APEX'
  A22 'RATING-SERVICE-COMET'
  A23 'RATING-SPECIALS-COMET'
  A24 'RATING-PRICES-COMET'
  A25 'RATING-LOCATION-COMET'
  A26 'RATING-HOURS-COMET'
  A27 'RATING-SERVICE-ONE HOUR'
  A28 'RATING-SPECIALS-ONE HOUR'
  A29 'RATING-PRICES-ONE HOUR'
  A30 'RATING-LOCATION-ONE HOUR'
  A31 'RATING-HOURS-ONE HOUR'
  A32 'IMPORTANCE-SERVICE'
  A33 'IMPORTANCE-SPECIALS'
  A34 'IMPORTANCE-PRICES'
  A35 'IMPORTANCE-LOCATION'
  A36 'IMPORTANCE-HOURS'
  A37 'SEX OF RESPONDENT'
  A38 'AGE OF RESPONDENT'
  A39 'MARITAL STATUS'
  A40 'SIZE OF HOUSEHOLD'
  A41 'OCCUPATION'
  A42 'FAMILY INCOME'
  A11X 'DRY CLEANING SPENDING - RESCALED'
  A12X 'LAUNDRY SPENDING - RESCALED'
  SPENDTOT 'TOTAL SPENDING - DRY CLEANING + LAUNDRY'
  A16X 'DISTANCE FROM APEX - RESCALED'
  MOST 'DRY CLEANERS USED MOST OFTEN'
  DIST 'DUMMY FOR DISTANCE FROM APEX'
  A38X 'RESPONDENT AGE - RESCALED'
  A42X 'RESPONDENT INCOME - RESCALED'
```

```
VALUE LABELS
   A1 TO A4 1 'UNAIDED' 2 'AIDED' 3 'UNAWARE' 8 'RFSD OR DK'/
   A5 TO A8 1 'YES' 2 'NO' /
   A9 A10 1 'HIGH QUALITY' 2 'EXTRA CARE' 3 'ALL COUPONS'
       4 'SPECIALS' 5 'FRIENDLY SERVICE' 6 'VALUE-Q VS PRICE'
       7 'SPECIALTY ITEMS' 88 'RFSD OR DK' 99 'NOT APP'/
   A11 A12 1 'LESS TH $10' 2 '$11-$20' 3 '$21-$35'
           4 '$35-$50'  5 '$50-$75' 6 '$75-$100'
           7 'MORE TH $100' 8 'RFDS OR DK'/
   A13 1 'YES' 2 'NO' 8 'REFUSED OR DK'/
   A14 1 'PRICE OFF' 2 'SUITS'
           3 'SLACKS' 4 'SHIRTS & BLS' 8 'REFUSED OR DK'
           9 'NOT APP'/
   A15 1 'APEX' 2 'COMET' 3 'ONE HOUR'
       4 'OTHER' 8 'REFUSED OR DK'/
   A16 1 'LESS TH 1 MILE' 2 '1 TO < 2 MI'
       3 '2 TO < 3 MI' 4 '3 TO <  MI' 5 '5 MILES OR >'
       8 'REFUSED OR DK'/
   A17 TO A31 1 'EXCELLENT' 2 'GOOD' 3 'FAIR'
               4 'POOR' 8 'REFUSED OR DK'/
   A32 TO A36 1 'EXTREMELY' 2 'VERY' 3 'SOMEWHAT'
               4 'NOT IMP' 8 'REFUSED OR DK' /
   A37 1 'MALE' 2 'FEMALE'/
   A38 1 'UNDER 21' 2 '21 TO 35' 3 '26 TO 35'
       4 '36 TO 49' 5 '50 TO 69' 6 '70 OR OLDER'
       8 'REFUSED OR DK'/
   A39  1 'SINGLE' 2 'MARRIED' 3 'SEP, DIV, WIDOW'
       8 'REFUSED OR DK'/
   A40 8 'RFSD OR DK'/
   A41 1 'STUDENT' 2 'BLUE COLLAR' 3 'CLER,SALES,SKLD'
       4 'MANAGER-OWNER' 5 'PROFESSIONAL' 6 'OTHER'
       7 'UNEMPLOYED' 8 'RFSD OR DK'/
   A42  1 '$15,000 OR <' 2 '15,001 TO $25,000'
       3 '$25,001 TO $40,000' 4 '$40,001 TO $60,000'
       5 '$60,001 TO $100,000' 6 'OVER $100,000'
       8 'REFUSED OR DK'/
   DIST 1 '2 OR LESS MILES' 2 '3 OR MORE MILES'/
   MOST 1 'APEX' 2 'OTHER'
MISSING VALUES A1 TO A8 (0,8) A9 A10 (88,99,0) A11 TO A42 (8,9,0)
BEGIN DATA
     (Data Set Goes Here)
END DATA
FREQUENCIES VARIABLES = ALL/
   STATISTICS MEAN SEMEAN STDDEV
CROSSTABS TABLES = A16 BY A15
OPTIONS 2 3 4 5
STATISTICS 1
CROSSTABS TABLES = A16 BY A15
OPTIONS 2 3
STATISTICS 1
CROSSTABS TABLES = A15 BY A1 TO A4
OPTIONS 2 3
```

```
STATISTICS 1
BREAKDOWN A16X BY A15
CROSSTABS TABLES = DIST BY MOST
STATISTICS 1
OPTIONS 2 3
BREAKDOWN A1 TO A42 A11X A12X SPENDTOT A16X A38X A42X BY MOST
FREQUENCIES VARIABLES = A16X/
  STATISTICS MEAN SEMEAN STDDEV
BREAKDOWN A16X BY MOST
FINISH
```

Each question in the questionnaire represents one or more pieces of information (depending upon whether it is a single or multiple-response question). Each piece of information is identified within the program by a variable name. Variable names can be short (even a single letter will do) or up to eight characters long. They must begin with an alphabetic character and they may contain letters and numbers. Numbers have been used to identify the variable names in this example (i.e. A1 through A42). If you decide to not provide labels for your questions and answers (to be discussed shortly) you may choose to use more descriptive names for your variables. (e.g. RCLAPEX for recall of Apex, ADVAPEX for advertising for APEX)

It is not necessary to specify each and every variable name when the variables end in numbers. You may use the word "TO" to specify them. A1 TO A10 is equivalent to specifying A1 A2 A3 A4 A5 A6 A7 A8 A9 A10.

After a variable or list of variables, you specify the record column(s) from which the data is to be read. In the above example, the program will not read any data out of columns 1 through 4. These columns contain the interview ID number and the record ID. The numbers in these columns merely serve to identify the interview number and the line of the set of multiple records. Later, if you need to locate a data record in the file, this information may be useful. Variables A1 through A10 will be read out of the next ten columns (5 through 14). Variable A11 is a two-digit variable read from columns 15 and 16. When you specify several variables as a group, the number of columns assigned must be evenly divisible by the number of variables in the group. Variables A1 to A10 represent ten variables and will be read out of ten columns. (Had you specified, say, nine or eleven columns, you would get an error message.) Note that variables A16 and A17 are read out of four columns. The program will interpret this to mean that each variable is a two-digit variable.

The second record for each respondent begins after the /2 characters. On this second record, the interview and record IDs are again not read. Therefore, columns 1 through 4 are skipped. However, twenty variables (A21 through A40) will be read out of twenty consecutive columns (columns 5-24).

Note also in our example **DATA LIST** that the second program line does not begin in column 1. This tells the program to treat this line as continuations of the first line.

When you run the SPSS program, the output will provide you a listing of the variable names and the records and columns from which they will be read immediately after it reprints your **DATA LIST** command. You should carefully go through the listing to make sure that each piece of information is read from the proper column and record.

BEGIN DATA and **END DATA** Statements. It would be possible to run our example program with only a few more command lines. Two required lines are:

```
BEGIN DATA
  (Data set)
END DATA
```

The **BEGIN DATA** line tells the program that the statements that follow are not SPSS statements but are actual lines of data (from the data set you created from the questionnaires). Insert the **END DATA** line after all the data lines to tell the program to stop reading data and to resume processing SPSS statements. You may include as many lines of data as you wish, from a small number (for instance five lines to run a test of the program) to, literally, hundreds of thousands. In fact, you can run the program with no data at all to get an error check.

Following the **END DATA** line you place additional SPSS commands that direct the program to perform various procedures on your data, such as tabulations and cross-tabulations. We will discuss these procedures in Chapter Eight.

Labeling of Questions and Responses. Some additional statements that you might want to include in your program are the **VARIABLE LABELS** and **VALUE LABELS**. These two procedures tell the program to place the text of the questions and answers on the printed output when SPSS procedures are performed. This labeling can be very valuable when the time comes to read and interpret your printouts. Without it, the printout will only contain variable names and the numerical codes which identify the responses.   You will have to constantly refer to your questionnaire to determine which question was associated with the variable and which answers are associated with the coded responses. This is not only inconvenient but is also a potential source of error in transposition and interpretation.

VARIABLE LABELS correspond to the text of the questions, while **VALUE LABELS** correspond to the text of the answers. For example:

```
VARIABLE LABELS
      A1 'RECALL OF APEX'
      A2 'RECALL OF COMET'
      A3 'RECALL OF ONE HOUR'
      A4 'RECALL OF OTHERS'
```

The above command will cause the program to associate labels with each of the variables. These labels are limited to forty characters in length, so you may have to use some creativity in abbreviating the text of the question. You may have only one **VARIABLE LABELS** statement, but you may continue the command for as many lines as necessary to provide all your value labels.

```
VALUE LABELS
   A1 TO A4 1 'UNAIDED' 2 'AIDED' 3 'UNAWARE'/
   A5 TO A8 1 'YES' 2 'NO' /
   A11 A12 1 'LESS TH $10' 2 '$11-$20' 3 '$21-$35'
            4 '$35-$50'  5 '$50-$75' 6 '$75-$100'
            7 'MORE TH $100' 8 'RFDS OR DK'/
```

The set of lines above causes the text of the answers to each question to be associated with its respective variable. The name of the variable (or list of variables) comes first. Next, each answer code is listed. After the code, a space is skipped and the text of the answer is provided, enclosed in single quotation marks. The text of the answer cannot exceed sixteen characters in length, so careful abbreviation may be required (e.g., Refused or Don't Know = RFSD OR DK). The codes and the answers may be continued onto as many lines as necessary. Once the codes and answers have been entered for each variable (or group of variables), a "/" is entered prior to specifying the labels for additional variables.

Variable Transformations. The first thing the SPSS program does is to read your input data and store it into the computer's memory. When you request procedures (e.g., tabulations) to be performed, it will operate on the stored data values. Initially, the data that is stored is exactly the same as the data in your data set. However, it is possible to transform this data or to add new variables to the data set. These new variables are usually combinations of the original variables or are related to them in some way.

An important type of variable transformation is the **COMPUTE** statement. The **COMPUTE** statement allows you to create new variables based upon the values in the stored data set. These are new variables that were not specified on the **DATA LIST** statement. However, once they are created, they may be used just as any other variables.

Suppose we had two variables, A11X, "How much do you spend on laundry per month?" and A12X, "How much do you spend on dry cleaning per month?" Perhaps it would be useful to have an additional variable that would provide the total amount spent. The following statement could be used to create such a variable:

```
COMPUTE SPENDTOT = A11X + A12X
```

We have created a new variable that we have given the variable name SPENDTOT and it is the sum of the two variables A11X and A12X. In the **COMPUTE** statement, the original variables, A11X and A12X, are unaffected by this transformation. However, the new variable, SPENDTOT, is available to be used just as we use any of the variables read in on the original **DATA LIST.**

COMPUTE statements use mathematical operators to perform numerical operations on the variables. **COMPUTE** allows the use of all of the common arithmetical operations such as plus, minus, asterisk and slash to indicate addition, subtraction, multiplication and division.

They also allow a wide variety of more complex mathematical functions, such as logarithms and exponentiation (see the SPSS manual for a complete discussion).

Another very useful transformation is the **IF** statement. This statement can be used in a variety of ways. One convenient use for the **IF** statement is to provide values for variables that are part of skip patterns. Suppose that we had the following two questions:

6.   Do you ever use dry cleaning coupons?

(18)

YES   1
NO (SKIP TO QUESTION 8)   2
REFUSED OR DON'T KNOW (SKIP TO QUESTION 8)   8

7.   When you use coupons, what one type do you most prefer. Would it be (READ LIST BELOW)?

(19)

Price Off 1
Special prices on dry cleaning items   2
Special Prices on Laundry items   3
REFUSED OR DON'T KNOW 8

If the interviewers follow the instructions exactly, a NO or REFUSED response on Question Six would cause a skip to Question Eight. Thus, there would be no reason to enter a coded response to Question Seven. Perhaps, later, we might decide that we would like the not applicable responses identified with a special code, say code 9. Of course, this Code 9 could be recorded in the editing process and entered during the data entry process. However, the SPSS **IF** statement provides a simple way to ensure this coding of Question Seven.

```
IF (A13 NE 1) A14 = 9
```

Note that the **IF** statement has two parts, a condition (A13 NE 1) and a result (A14 = 9). If the condition is True, (Code 1 not entered for A13) the result is executed. If the condition is False (Code 1 entered for A13), then the result is ignored and not executed. Note also that the condition uses **logical** operators. Some of the logical operators that can be used in a condition are:

OPERATOR	MEANING
EQ	Equal to
GT	Greater than
LT	Less than
GE	Greater than or equal to
LE	Less than or equal to
NE	Not equal to
AND	Joins two conditions
OR	Statement is true if either part before or after the OR is true

Note also that the result following the condition is not a logical operator but rather an arithmetic operator. In essence, the result portion of the **IF** statement is equivalent to the **COMPUTE** statement. However, the computation is performed only if the conditional is true.

Another way that the **IF** statement is often used is to create new variables from the variables that were originally entered as a part of the data set. This may be done to create pseudo-interval variables which will have some of the qualities of true interval variables. You may recall from your textbook that the arithmetic mean may only properly be calculated from interval data. Nevertheless, the data you enter into your data set is usually nominal or ordinal. The original codes and the responses for variable A16 ("How far is Apex from your home?") are presented below:

Code	Response
1	Less than one mile
2	One to less than two miles
3	Two to less than three miles
4	Three to less than five miles
5	Five miles or more

If you request that the program calculate the mean for variable A16, it would calculate the mean of the *codes*. These codes bear a rough relationship to the distance the respondent lives from the store. However, an average coded value of, for instance, 2.63 would be difficult to interpret. The codes can be transformed into a better representation of distance.

Suppose that you were able to know the exact distance from the store for all those who responded "Less than one mile." What do you suppose would be the average distance for these respondents? Most people would probably guess that the average distance is somewhere around one-half mile. For those in the second category, a good estimate would be 1.5 miles. You would probably use 2.5 miles for those in the third category. The top category presents a bit of a problem since it has no upper bound. But if you assume that people are not likely to travel great distances to a dry cleaning establishment, you might estimate that the average distance within this highest group is 6.0 miles.

You can use the following **IF** statements to create a new variable (we will call it A16X) with these transformed values:

```
IF (A16 EQ 1) A16X = .5
IF (A16 EQ 2) A16X = 1.5
IF (A16 EQ 3) A16X = 2.5
IF (A16 EQ 4) A16X = 4.0
IF (A16 EQ 5) A16X = 6.0
```

When the above statements are encountered, the program will go through all the stored values for variable A16 in the internal data set, test them, and assign the appropriate value to variable A16X according to which **IF** statement is true. Note that in our example program (Table 7B.1) we have added variable A16X to our **VALUE LABELS** set so that it may be easily identified when we use it later in an SPSS procedure.

Another common type of variable transformation is the **RECODE** statement, which may be thought of as a compound **IF** statement. The purpose of **RECODE** is to change the values that are stored in memory. For instance, in our Apex example, suppose we had two dry cleaners (M Cleaners-Code 4, and Vogue-Code 5) as well as an OTHER category (Code 6). Suppose that there were very few Code 4 and 5 responses and we wanted to assign them to the other category to simplify our output and analysis. The following **IF** statements could be used:

```
IF  (A15  EQ  4)A15  =  6
IF  (A15  EQ  5)A15  =  6
```

A more compact form of the above statements would be:

```
IF  (A15  EQ  4  OR  A15  EQ  5)A15  =  6
```

However, the **RECODE** statement provides an even simpler method of performing these transformations:

```
RECODE  A15  (4,5=6)
```

The effect of the above command would be to change all of the Codes 4 and 5 in the stored data set (not in your input data set) to Code 6. Thus, the output resulting from any procedures would not contain any Code 4s or 5s and the size of the OTHER category (Code 6) would increase.

You can recode multiple values in the same command, as we did above. You can also recode several variables at the same time. For instance, the above command could have been:

```
RECODE  A1,  A12,  A22  to  A29  (4,5=6)
```

Recall that in our example of creating pseudo-interval data, we used the values of variable A16 to create a new variable called A16X. If we were not concerned with keeping the original values of A16 intact, we could simply recode the values of variable A16 with the following **RECODE** statement.

```
RECODE   A16  (1=.5)  (2=1.5)  (3=2.5)(4=4.0)(5=6.0)
```

When the above statement is encountered, the program will go through all the stored values for variable A16 in the internal data set and change them to the new values. When the mean is calculated, it will be the mean of the recoded values. One word of caution is in order regarding **VALUE LABELS** for recoded variables. Once a variable has been transformed into a new set of codes, these are the codes that will be printed out when requesting frequency distributions. Thus, these new codes are the ones that must be used when assigning value labels to the recoded variables.

Another use of the **RECODE** statement is to change missing values to other values. When SPSS reads a blank column, it automatically assigns a code called the "system missing value." This value will always be treated as a missing value unless you change it to something else with a statement such as the following:

```
RECODE A1 TO A4 (SYSMIS=3)
```

When the above statement is encountered, all the system missing values will be changed to code 3s. (SYSMIS is the name that SPSS uses to refer to system missing values). These code 3s will not be treated as missing unless you assign them as missing in the **MISSING VALUES** statement which we will discuss next.

Missing Values Statement. In Chapter Eight, we will discuss some of the common types of SPSS procedures that you will use in your data analysis. Each of these procedures will treat "missing values" differently than "nonmissing" values. We mentioned missing values in Chapter Five in our discussion of questionnaire design. There are several ways of assigning values as missing. When SPSS reads the data set, any column that is left blank or into which is entered a single period (.) will be treated automatically as a missing value. Sometimes you will want to designate specific responses, such as "Refused" or "Not Applicable" as missing values. Consider the following question:

8.   **Which dry cleaners do you use most often?**

(20)

APEX	1
COMET	2
ONE HOUR	3
OTHER SPECIFY_____ .... ____	
REFUSED OR DON'T KNOW	8

In the above example, the computer would treat the code 8s in the same way as any other values. However, if want percentages based upon the percent of meaningful responses, we would like to leave them out of the calculation entirely. This is done by designating them as missing on a **MISSING VALUES** statement:

```
MISSING VALUES A15 (0,8)
```

There can be only one **MISSING VALUES** statement in your program. However, it may specify the missing values for all the variables in your data set (including those created by variable transformations). A typical missing values statement is:

```
MISSING VALUES A1 TO A8 (0) A9 A10 (88,99,0)
     A11 TO A42 (8,9,0)
```

All variables with the same missing values are grouped together. Just after each group of variables, all the missing values for that group are enclosed in parentheses.

Other Command Lines. There are at least two other statements that you will want to include in your program. The first of these is the **FINISH** statement which includes only the word **FINISH** (beginning in column 1) and should be the very last line of your program (after any SPSS procedures you perform on a particular run of the program).

Another useful statement is **PRINT FORMATS**. This statement is only needed if you have noninteger values in your data set. All of your data will probably be entered into the data set as integers (that is, without decimal points) when using the fixed record format we have suggested. In SPSS output, the codes would, therefore, be presented as integers. However, note that in the recoding of distance above, we created some decimal codes (e.g., .5, 1.5, 4.0, 6.0). In order for these codes to appear properly in our printed output, we need to add the following statement:

```
PRINT FORMATS A16 (F4.1)
```

This tells the program that variable A2 will now appear in the output as a decimal number with up to four digits and one digit after the decimal point. As with the **MISSING VALUES** statement, you may specify several variables on one **PRINT FORMATS** line.

Order of Command Lines. Most of the command lines used in SPSS will refer to variables in the data set. Many procedures, such as **VARIABLE LABELS** and **VALUE LABELS** will work only with variables that have previously been created. We have discussed some of the most common ways of creating SPSS variables:

1.   Listing them on the **DATA LIST** command and entering them as part of the data set.

2.   Creating them with the **IF** statement, the **COMPUTE** statement or some other variable transformation.

Thus, the above methods must be used to create variables before they are referred to in procedures that will use them. If you refer to a variable in any statement (e.g., **VARIABLE LABELS**) and it has not been previously created in one of the above ways, you will get an error message stating "UNKNOWN VARIABLE NAME." A typical SPSS program presents statements in the following order:

```
System Control Lines
TITLE
DATA LIST
IF, RECODE, AND COMPUTE statements
VARIABLE LABELS
VALUE LABELS
PRINT FORMATS
MISSING VALUES statement
BEGIN DATA
      (data set)
END DATA
      (SPSS Procedures)
FINISH statement
```

SPSS Error Messages. A host of errors might be made in an SPSS program, and at least on the first few tests of your program, you are almost certain to see some of them. The more common errors include:

1.   Error in system statements. This is usually indicated when you do not get back anything that resembles an SPSS program. Usually, when a system error is encountered, an immediate error message is issued and none of the remainder of the program is processed. System statements provide instructions to your computer system. They are not a part of the SPSS procedures. They are commonly placed before any part of your SPSS program. Usually, when a system error is encountered, an immediate error message is issued and none of the remainder of the program is processed. Since no SPSS statements are processed, no SPSS output is produced.

2.   Errors on the **DATA LIST** statement. Providing more or fewer data columns than required by a group of variables will cause this error. Even if the **DATA LIST** statement does not cause an error, you should check your data format against the column assignments indicated on the SPSS output. The listing of column assignments will appear on your output just after the **DATA LIST** statement.

3.   Unrecognized keywords. All keywords (e.g., **TITLE, DATA LIST**, and **VALUE LABELS**) must be spelled correctly to be recognized by the program. Keywords must begin in column 1.

4.   Unknown variable. This occurs when a variable name is encountered that has not been previously created by the **DATA LIST** or a variable transformation.

5.   Errors in punctuation. On the **VARIABLE LABELS** statement, the label itself

is enclosed in single quotation marks. It is easy to leave off the terminating quotation mark. A "/" indicates the beginning of a set of labels for a new variable.

6.   No **BEGIN DATA** or **END DATA** statement. **BEGIN DATA** tells the program to begin reading data from your data set. If it were left out, the program would attempt to read lines of the data set as program statements. This would cause an error since they do not begin with keywords. On the other hand, if the **END DATA** statement is left off the end of the data, program statements would be treated as though they were part of the data set. Usually this causes a series of errors when the alphabetic characters of the statement are not recognized as numbers.

CHAPTER EIGHT
DATA ANALYSIS

Data analysis is a key step in the marketing research process. Several chapters of your marketing research textbook cover this topic, and entire textbooks and courses are devoted to specific aspects, such as multivariate analysis. In this chapter, we will highlight some of the common analysis procedures that are applicable to nearly any data set that might be generated.

RUNNING SAS PROCEDURES

If you have followed the steps suggested in Chapter Seven, you should have a SAS or SPSS program to which you will add various analysis procedures. In this chapter, we will examine the SAS procedures **FREQUENCIES** and **MEANS**. We will also provide the equivalent SPSS commands to generate SPSS output. Chapter Nine will illustrate the use of these procedures in preparing the research report. In Chapter Ten, you will find some example setups for such multivariate procedures as regression, discriminant analysis, and cluster analysis.

Normally, any SAS procedures you request will be placed at the end of your program. When you request a new procedure, do not forget to take the old procedure statements out. Otherwise, they will be run again along with the newly requested procedures, adding unnecessary additional lines to your output.

It is possible to run as many procedures as you like on any given SAS run. The only constraint is the maximum amount of computer time or the maximum number of lines of output your system allows and/or job setup requests a single run. There will usually be some amount of default time or lines allowed for each job in a batch-processing computer environment. Usually these default values are large enough to run several SAS procedures, particularly when data sets are small. The system may also allow you to override the default values through the specification of parameters on system control statements, but this can cause your job to be assigned a lower priority and may affect the turnaround time.

GENERAL FLOW OF DATA ANALYSIS

Good data analysis proceeds in stages, and often it is difficult to specify the procedures in the next stage until you see the results from the previous one. Therefore, our discussion will progress, in order, through the stages typically encountered in analyzing marketing research data.

One of the most important goals in analyzing marketing research data is summarizing. Your data set contains literally thousands of pieces of numerical information that must be summarized into a smaller set of numbers (percentages, means, and other statistics) that will present the essential meaning behind the data. As a general rule, you want to present your results in the simplest form that will support the conclusions suggested by your data.

THE FREQUENCIES PROCEDURE - ONE-WAY DISTRIBUTIONS

The most common procedure any tabulation program performs is frequency counts of the responses to each question. The following SAS statement, placed at the end of your program, will request a frequency distribution of all the variables in the data set (see the example job setup for the exact placement of procedure statements):

```
PROC FREQ DATA=CLEANERS;
```

```
SPSS PROCEDURE - Place just after the END DATA statement:

     FREQUENCIES VARIABLES=ALL/
       STATISTICS MEAN STDDEV SEMEAN
```

You may be surprised to find that the one SAS statement listed above will generate a considerable amount of output. If there are 40 variables in your data set, you will get at least 40 tables of output. **PROC FREQ** will generate a separate table for each variable in your data set.

In Chapter Seven we showed you how to create formats for labeling the responses to your questions. In order to add a title and to associate these formats with your output, the **PROC FREQ** should be prepared as follows:

```
PROC FREQ DATA=CLEANERS;
     TITLE2 'SAS FREQUENCY DISTRIBUTIONS';
     FORMAT A1--A4 RCLFMT. A5--A8 ADFMT.
          A11 A12 SPENDFMT. A13 YESNOFMT. A14 CPNFMT.
          A15 MOSTFMT. A16 DISTFMT. A17--A31 RATEFMT.
          A32--A36 IMPFMT. A37 SEXFMT. A38 AGEFMT.
          A39 MSTATFMT. A42 INCFMT.;
```

> SPSS Procedure - **FORMAT** statements are not required. Labeling of
> questions and responses will be automatically provided if **VARIABLE
> LABELS** and **VALUE LABELS** were specified in the program setup.

Within the **PROC FREQ** step, you add the **FORMAT** statement which provides the names
of the variables (or groups of variables) for which you are requesting frequencies. These
variables or groups of variables are followed by the name of the format that will be
associated with them. This format name is one of the formats that you created in the **PROC
FORMAT** statement we discussed in Chapter Seven. Note that a period (.) is added to the
end of each of these format names. Note also that, because you have created two data sets
during the SAS run (CLEANERS AND LABELSET), it is necessary to identify the name
of the data set on the **PROC FREQ**.

If you do not request tables for specific variables on the **PROC FREQ**, SAS will generate
a table for all of the variables in the data set, both those that were input as well as those
generated by variable transformations. However, if you want frequency tables only for
specific variables, you may add a **TABLES** request to the **PROC FREQ** step:

```
PROC FREQ DATA=CLEANERS;
     TITLE2 'SAS FREQUENCY DISTRIBUTIONS';
     FORMAT A1--A4 RCLFMT. A15 MOSTFMT. A16 DISTFMT.;
     TABLES = A1--A4 A15 A16;
```

> SPSS PROCEDURE - Place just after the **END DATA** statement:
>
> **FREQUENCIES** VARIABLES = A1 TO A4 A15 A16/
> **STATISTICS** = MEAN STDDEV SEMEAN
>
> (lists of variables are specified by joining them with the word TO)

The **PROC FREQ** above would generate a table for A1, A2, A3, A4, A4, A15, and A16.
Note particularly the usage of the double hyphen in "A1--A4": this indicates that all variables
listed on the **DATA** statement between A1 and A4 are to be included.

A typical table of output from the frequencies procedure for variable A15 would appear as follows:

APEX DRY CLEANING STUDY

WHAT DRY CLEANERS DO YOU USE MOST OFTEN?

A15	FREQUENCY	PERCENT	CUMULATIVE FREQUENCY	CUMULATIVE PERCENT
REFUSED OR DK	11	.	.	.
APEX	65	34.4	65	34.4
COMET	69	36.5	134	70.9
ONE HOUR	43	22.8	177	93.7
OTHER	12	6.3	189	100.0

The interpretation of the above table is straightforward. At the top of the table is the title. The next line is the label associated with the variable for which the table is being generated. On the first line of the table is the name of the variable, followed by headings for each of the columns. Response labels (as they were provided in the **FORMAT** statement) appear in the first column of the table. The next column contains the frequency count for each response, that is, the number of times it was found in the data set. We see that there eleven subjects who did not provide a response to the question and sixty-five subjects who responded that they use Apex most often. The "Percent" column tells us that these sixty-five responses represented 34.4 percent of the total of the valid (nonmissing) responses. There were only 189 valid responses (the eleven "REFUSED OR DON'T KNOW" responses have been treated as missing). Thus, percentages are calculated leaving them out of the divisor. No percentages are calculated for the "REFUSED OR DON'T KNOW" category and a period appears for the last three columns. The next column presents the cumulative frequencies, that is, the number of responses indicated by the respective code and all codes of lower value. The final column converts these cumulative frequencies into percentages of the total nonmissing values.

THE MEANS PROCEDURE-SIMPLE MEANS

Numerical Variables. The table presented above provides an example of categorical data. The codes entered into the computer did nothing more than uniquely identify each response. We associated the response "Apex" with code 1. However, it would have been equally appropriate to assign it some other coded value. There are only a few statistical measures that may be used to summarize categorical data into a simpler form. Percentages and modes are among the statistical measures that are readily applicable to this type of data.

Some variables in your data set are likely to have numerical qualities. In other words, the categories are ordered from low to high. Low values of the variable indicate small quantities of what has been measured, while larger values indicate greater amounts. Numerical variables may be summarized by summary statistics in addition to percentages and modes. Consider the following frequency table from the variable A16 ("How far is Apex from your home?").

APEX DRY CLEANING STUDY

HOW FAR IS APEX FROM YOUR HOME?

A16	FREQUENCY	PERCENT	CUMULATIVE FREQUENCY	CUMULATIVE PERCENT
RFSD OR DK	9	.	.	.
LESS TH 1 MILE	23	12.0	23	12.0
1 TO < 2 MILES	50	26.2	73	38.2
2 TO < 3 MILES	65	34.0	138	72.3
3 TO < 5 MILES	40	20.9	178	93.2
5 MILES OR MORE	13	6.8	191	100.0

Clearly, the frequency counts and percentages are useful in providing us with an indication of the proximity of customers to Apex's store. However, recall that, in Chapter Seven, through the use of **IF** statements, we used variable A16 to create the "pseudo-interval" variable A16X so that each code represented the average distance for all of the subjects in the group. A numerical variable may be summarized into its mean and standard deviation. Furthermore, the standard error of the mean helps us determine the confidence we can place in these statistics. **PROC MEANS** is a SAS procedure for producing these statistical measures.

> **PROC MEANS** DATA=CLEANERS;
> **VAR** A16X;

> SPSS Procedure: Statistics for each variable are automatically provided by the **STATISTICS** request included in the **FREQUENCIES** procedure.

If you do not use the **VAR** statement, all variables in your data set will be analyzed. The PROC listed above would produce the following output:

VARIABLE	N	MEAN	STANDARD DEVIATION	MINIMUM VALUE	MAXIMUM VALUE	STD ERROR OF MEAN	SUM	VARIANCE
A16X	191	2.549738	1.434128	.500000	6.000000	.103770	487.000000	2.056724

Each line of output from **PROC MEANS** provides:

the name of the VARIABLE
N, the number of nonmissing observations
the MEAN, or average, of the variable
the STANDARD DEVIATION of the variable
the MINIMUM VALUE of the variable
the MAXIMUM VALUE of the variable
the STD ERROR OF THE MEAN
the SUM of the values for a variable
the VARIANCE of each variable

All of the above statistics are sampling estimates of the population values, and each is calculated based upon the nonmissing values in the data set.

Confidence Intervals. The mean, ($\bar{x}$) and the standard error ($\hat{s}_{\bar{x}}$) are of particular interest. The mean is a true summary measure and represents an estimate of the most likely value of the variable that would be found in the population. The standard error provides an indication of how much confidence may be placed in this estimate of the mean. Using these two statistics, you may construct an interval that is likely to contain the true mean of the population with some desired level of confidence:

From our example **PROC FREQ**, this interval may be constructed as:

$$\bar{x} - Z \, \hat{s}_{\bar{x}} < \mu < \bar{x} + Z \, \hat{s}_{\bar{x}}$$

$$2.550 - 1.96 \, (.1038) < \mu < 2.550 + 1.96 \, (.1038)$$

95 Percent Confidence Interval of A16X (Distance from Apex)

$$2.347 < \mu < 2.753$$

In discussing the interpretation of the statistics related to A16, "distance from Apex," in your research report, you may list the confidence interval as we have done above, or you may prefer to simply use a statement such as:

> Of the people who responded to this question, the average distance from Apex was 2.550 miles. Given a sample size of 191, we are 95 percent confident that this is within .203 miles of the true value for the population.

The .203 mile interval in the above statement is equal to 1.96 (the Z value) times .1038 (the standard error of the estimate of the mean).

FREQUENCIES PROCEDURE - CROSS-TABULATION

Frequency distributions and statistical measures are useful in providing the researcher with a picture of the population of interest. However, a serious analysis of a marketing research study will almost always go farther. Market segmentation, as a managerial strategy, is ultimately interested in characteristics of subgroups within the population. Subgroups of the sample could be defined in innumerable ways. Some typical subgroups of interest could include: males versus females, high-income versus low-income consumers, undergraduates versus graduate students, and buyers versus non buyers of the product. For each of these groups, the analyst will be interested in some, if not all, of the responses to the questions contained within the questionnaire. Cross-tabulation is a procedure for observing these differences between groups.

PROC FREQ allows for the convenient generation of cross-tabulation tables:

```
PROC FREQ DATA=CLEANERS;
     TITLE2 'SAS CROSS-TABULATIONS';
     FORMAT A15 MOSTFMT. A16 DISTFMT.;
     TABLES A16*A15/CHISQ;
```

```
SPSS Procedure:  Place just after the END DATA statement:


          CROSSTABS TABLES=A16 BY A15
          OPTIONS 2 3 4 5
          STATISTICS   1
```

This **PROC FREQ** requests a crosstabulation of variable A16 by variable A15. Note that, in the **TABLES** request, we have added the **CHISQ** option which requests that the Chi-Squared statistic be calculated for the table. We will tell you about the Chi-Square statistic after discussing the cross-tabulation table. The procedure described above would generate the following table:

TABLE OF A16 BY A15

A16 (HOW FAR IS APEX FROM YOUR HOME?)
          A15 (WHICH DRY CLEANERS DO YOU USE MOST OFTEN?)

```
FREQUENCY
PERCENT
ROW PCT
COL PCT        |APEX   |COMET  |ONE HOUR| OTHER |  TOTAL
---------------+-------+-------+--------+-------+
LESS TH 1 MILE |   16  |    3  |    2   |    0  |    21
               |  8.84 |  1.66 |  1.10  |  0.00 |  11.60
               | 76.19 | 14.29 |  9.52  |  0.00 |
               | 25.40 |  4.62 |  4.88  |  0.00 |
---------------+-------+-------+--------+-------+
1 TO < 2 MI    |   21  |   13  |   11   |    3  |    48
               | 11.60 |  7.18 |  6.08  |  1.66 |  26.52
               | 43.75 | 27.08 | 22.92  |  6.25 |
               | 33.33 | 20.00 | 26.83  | 25.00 |
---------------+-------+-------+--------+-------+
2 TO < 3 MI    |   19  |   25  |   13   |    3  |    60
               | 10.50 | 13.81 |  7.18  |  1.66 |  33.15
               | 31.67 | 41.67 | 21.67  |  5.00 |
               | 30.16 | 38.46 | 31.71  | 25.00 |
---------------+-------+-------+--------+-------+
3 TO < 5  MI   |    4  |   18  |   11   |    6  |    39
               |  2.21 |  9.94 |  6.08  |  3.31 |  21.55
               | 10.26 | 46.15 | 28.21  | 15.38 |
               |  6.35 | 27.69 | 26.83  | 50.00 |
---------------+-------+-------+--------+-------+
5 MILES OR >   |    3  |    6  |    4   |    0  |    13
               |  1.66 |  3.31 |  2.21  |  0.00 |   7.18
               | 23.08 | 46.15 | 30.77  |  0.00 |
               |  4.76 |  9.23 |  9.76  |  0.00 |
---------------+-------+-------+--------+-------+
TOTAL              63      65      41       12     181
                 34.81   35.91   22.65    6.63   100.00
```

FREQUENCY MISSING = 19

STATISTICS FOR TABLE OF A16 BY A15

STATISTIC	DF	VALUE	PROB
CHI-SQUARE	12	34.270	0.001

The cross-tabulation presented above includes all the categories of A16 and A15 except those that have been identified as missing. Thus the above table has twenty "cells," defined by five rows and four columns. In the margins (bottom and right hand sides) of the table, we find the total frequencies for each of the categories of the two variables. The right hand column of the table indicates that there were twenty-one people who live within one mile of Apex, and these respondents represent 11.6 percent of all of the respondents. Along the bottom of the table, we find the frequencies for variable A15. Sixty-three of the respondents (34.81 percent) say that they use Apex most often. The bottom right hand corner of the table tells us that the table contains 181 total responses. Note that the marginal frequencies are nearly identical to those produced by **PROC FREQ** to generate separate frequency distributions for each variable. However, missing values are not now included in the table and, if a subject has a missing value on either of the variables, that subjects' responses are excluded from the table. This has reduced our original sample size of 200 to 181.

Each cell of the table contains four pieces of information. A legend to these entries is provided in the uppermost left hand corner of the table. In each cell, the first line presents the frequency of the cell. This is a joint frequency of occurrence of respondents in that cell. The first cell of the above table indicates that there were sixteen respondents who use Apex most often *and* live within one mile of Apex. The next cell to the right tells us that there are three respondents who live within one mile of Apex and use Comet as their most preferred cleaners.

The second row of each cell presents the "total percent." The total percent is the cell frequency divided by the total of the frequencies in the entire table, in this case, sixteen divided by 181 or 8.44 percent. The third row of each cell presents the row percent, the frequency in the cell divided by the total frequency for the row. For the first cell, this is sixteen divided by twenty-one, or 76.19 percent. The bottom row of each cell is the column percent. It is the frequency in the cell divided by the total frequency in the column; in the case of the first cell, sixteen divided by sixty-three, or 25.4 percent.

The table above represents a complete output from **PROC FREQ**. It is also possible to obtain simpler tables that do not provide as much information.

```
PROC FREQ DATA=CLEANERS;
     TABLES A16*A15/CHISQ NOPERCENT NOCOL;
```

> SPSS Procedure - Place just after the **END DATA** statement:
>
> ```
> CROSSTABS TABLES = A16 BY A15
> STATISTICS 1
> OPTIONS 2 3
> ```
>
> (For column percents, specify **OPTIONS** 4. For total percents, specify **OPTIONS** 5)

The NOPERCENT and NOCOL options cause the total percentages and the column percentages to be eliminated from the table (NOFREQ and NOROW would eliminate the frequencies and the row percents, respectively). The row variable is the one placed before the * on the **TABLES** request.

```
                      TABLE OF A16 BY A15

A16 (HOW FAR IS APEX FROM YOUR HOME?)
                    A15 (WHICH DRY CLEANERS DO YOU USE MOST OFTEN

FREQUENCY       |
ROW PCT         |APEX    |COMET   |ONE HOUR|     4|  TOTAL
----------------+--------+--------+--------+--------+
LESS TH 1 MILE  |   16   |    3   |    2   |    0  |    21
                | 76.19  | 14.29  |  9.52  |  0.00 |  11.60
----------------+--------+--------+--------+--------+
1 TO < 2 MI     |   21   |   13   |   11   |    3  |    48
                | 43.75  | 27.08  | 22.92  |  6.25 |  26.52
----------------+--------+--------+--------+--------+
2 TO < 3 MI     |   19   |   25   |   13   |    3  |    60
                | 31.67  | 41.67  | 21.67  |  5.00 |  33.15
----------------+--------+--------+--------+--------+
3 TO < 5  MI    |    4   |   18   |   11   |    6  |    39
                | 10.26  | 46.15  | 28.21  | 15.38 |  21.55
----------------+--------+--------+--------+--------+
5 MILES OR >    |    3   |    6   |    4   |    0  |    13
                | 23.08  | 46.15  | 30.77  |  0.00 |   7.18
----------------+--------+--------+--------+--------+
TOTAL               63       65       41       12     181
                  34.81    35.91    22.65     6.63   100.00

      FREQUENCY MISSING = 19

             STATISTICS FOR TABLE OF A16 BY A15
      STATISTIC              DF      VALUE      PROB
      ------------------------------------------------
      CHI-SQUARE             12     34.270     0.001
```

Often, it may be helpful to have to deal with only one set of percentages. This is because we are usually interested in the number of subjects in a given group who exhibit some type of activity, interest or opinion. This may be the case when one variable is thought of as the "causal" variable and the other as the "caused" variable. When this is the case, it is best to calculate the percentages in the direction of the causal variable. In other words, if the causal variable is placed on the row, we would prefer to present the row percentages. When tables are set up this way, it is easier to construct statement such as:

"Of the twenty-one respondents who live within one mile of Apex, 76 percent say they use Apex most often."

In this case, we are implying that distance may be an explanation for why people choose Apex. Clearly, the reverse statement would make little sense. It is unlikely that people have chosen to live near Apex because that is where they take their dry cleaning.

Note that the marginal percentages at the bottom of the table provide a basis for comparison of the other row percentages. For example, among all of the respondents, 34.81 percent of the use Apex most often. However, the first row of cells of the table reveals that, of those who live within one mile of Apex, 76.19 percent use Apex most often. For those living one or more but less than two miles from Apex, the percentage is 43.75. Only 23.08 percent of those living five or more miles from Apex choose Apex most often.

The Chi-Square Statistic. If distance were not important in choosing a dry cleaners, we would expect the percentages choosing Apex to be near the overall average regardless of the distance of Apex from the respondents. It would appear from the above table that the distance people live from Apex may provide at least a partial explanation for their choice of a dry cleaners. For those living close, the patronage percentage is well above the average. For those living farther away, the patronage percentage is below the average.

If the percentages of those choosing Apex were near the average, regardless of distance, we could conclude that distance from Apex is not a good explanation for why customers choose it most often. A statistician would refer to this condition as statistical independence. On the other hand, a large departure of the percentages from the average provides some evidence that these two variables may be related (not independent).

We would never expect the percentages in each category to be exactly equal to the average, if only because of sampling error. In other words, if we were to take several samples from a population using the same procedures, we would expect similar but not identical results. Suppose that the percentages depart from the averages by smaller amounts than we have observed in the above table. How large a departure from the average would we want to see in order to conclude that the variables are not independent? Such evidence is provided by the Chi-Square statistic. The Chi-Square statistic is calculated by comparing the actual frequencies in the cells with the frequencies that would be expected if the variables are independent. For instance, the first row of the table contains twenty-one respondents. Therefore, if the variables were independent, we would expect to find the respondents in this row choosing Apex with about the same likelihood as those in other rows. We could calculate this expected frequency by multiplying 34.81 percent times the twenty-one subjects in that row, getting about seven respondents. In fact, we note that sixteen subjects, over twice as many as expected, fall into this cell.

Larger and larger departures of the cell frequencies from their expected values indicate that something other than random error may be occurring. One likely cause is that the expected values are calculated by assuming that the variables are independent. Large departures of the cell frequencies from their expected values may indicate that the independence assumption is not supported by the actual data. The Chi-Square statistic is very useful in assessing the degree to which cell frequencies depart from their expected values (see your text for a more complete discussion of how the Chi-Square statistic is calculated). The more the cell frequencies depart from their expected values (assuming independence), the larger the Chi-Square value will become. For the above table, this value is 34.270. Since the Chi-Square value is calculated across all the cells of the table, larger tables naturally produce larger Chi-Square values. Thus, whether a Chi-Square value is large or not will depend upon the size of the table, and this is indicated by its degrees of freedom. The degrees of freedom for a table are calculated as:

d.f = (number of rows - 1) x (number of columns - 1)

In the above table, this is $(5 - 1) \times (4 - 1) = 12$. A table of Chi-Square values (found in an appendix of your marketing research or statistics textbook) would tell us that, in a table with 12 degrees of freedom, random error would cause a Chi-Square value of 34.270 or larger with a probability of less than .001 *if the variables are independent.* In other words, if the variables are independent a Chi-Square value this large would occur by chance less than one time in one thousand. This offers strong evidence that the assumption of independence is unwarranted. Therefore, the researcher can say that the distance people live from Apex is a possible cause of choosing Apex.

Multiple Tables. When using **PROC FREQ** for cross-tabulation, you can request several tables on a single run. Consider the following **PROC FREQ**:

```
PROC FREQ DATA=CLEANERS;
TITLE2 'SAS CROSS-TABULATIONS';
     FORMAT A1--A4 RCLFMT. A16 MOSTFMT.;
     TABLES A15*A1--A4/CHISQ NOCOL NOPERCENT;
```

```
SPSS Procedure - Place just after the END DATA statement:

     CROSSTABS TABLES = A15 BY A1 TO A4
     OPTIONS 2 3
     STATISTICS 1
```

In the **TABLES** request, you can place more than one variable on either side of the asterisk. This is equivalent to requesting a table for all the variables before the asterisk by all the variables after the asterisk. The **PROC** above is equivalent to requesting a table for A15*A1, A15*A2, A15*A3 and A15*A4.

MEANS PROCEDURE - GROUP VARIABLES

Earlier we introduced the **PROC MEANS** procedure as a method for calculating various statistical measures for the variables in the data set. **PROC MEANS** can also produce two-way (and n-way) tables. In the previous cross-tabulation table, we note that, of the sixty-three subjects who use Apex most often, sixteen live within one mile. Twenty-one live one to two miles from Apex, nineteen live from two to three miles away, four live three to five miles from Apex and three live more than five miles from Apex. There is also a similar frequency distribution for each of the three remaining establishments. A researcher might wonder, "How far does the average customer of each of the four establishments live from Apex?"

The following **PROC MEANS** can provide this information.

```
PROC MEANS DATA=CLEANERS;
VAR A16X;
PROC SORT DATA=CLEANERS;
     BY A15;
PROC MEANS DATA=CLEANERS;
     BY A15;
     VAR A16X;
```

> SPSS Procedure - Place just after the **END DATA** statement:
>
> **BREAKDOWN** A16X BY A15

Both of the **PROC** statements above could be requested on the same run. The first **PROC** would request a means computation across all the subjects for variable A16X. The **PROC SORT** statement causes SAS to sort the respondents into groups defined by variable A15 (the order of the input data set is unaffected). The next **PROC** requests a separate **MEANS** computation for each group of respondents identified by their response to variable A15.

The above **PROC MEANS** will produce statistics as follows:

VARIABLE	N	MEAN	STANDARD DEVIATION	MINIMUM VALUE	MAXIMUM VALUE	STD ERROR OF MEAN	SUM	VARIANCE
A16X	191	2.549738	1.434128	.500000	6.000000	.103770	487.000000	2.056724

VARIABLE	N	MEAN	STANDARD DEVIATION	MINIMUM VALUE	MAXIMUM VALUE	STD ERROR OF MEAN	SUM	VARIANCE

-------------------------------CLEANERS USED MOST OFTEN = . -------------------------------

A16X	10	2.050000	1.065885	.500000	6.000000	.337062	20.500000	1.136111

-------------------------------CLEANERS USED MOST OFTEN = 1 -------------------------------

A16X	63	1.920635	1.329584	.500000	6.000000	.167512	121.000000	1.767793

-------------------------------CLEANERS USED MOST OFTEN = 2 -------------------------------

A16X	65	2.946154	1.403464	.500000	6.000000	.174078	191.5000000	1.969712

-------------------------------CLEANERS USED MOST OFTEN = 3 -------------------------------

A16X	41	2.878049	1.473858	.500000	6.000000	.230178	118.000000	2.172256

------------------------------- CLEANERS USED MOST OFTEN = 4 -------------------------------

A16X	12	3.000000	1.107823	.500000	4.000000	.319801	36.000000	1.227273

In the above table, each line of output provides the statistics associated with **PROC MEANS.** The top of the table reproduces the **PROC MEANS** for the total sample discussed earlier. The next five segments of output provide the **PROC MEANS** statistics, but now broken down by each of the values of the variable A15. The first line provides statistics for the "missing" category of A15, that is, those respondents who expressed no preference. The next line is for the value of A15 equal to 1, those who said that they used Apex most often. The next line is for the value of A15 equal to 2, those who use Comet most often. For each group defined by variable A15, we have the **PROC MEANS** statistics. The above table tells us that those who use Apex most often live an average of 1.920635 miles from Apex. Those who use Comet most often live an average of 2.946154 miles from Apex, and so on.

SIMPLIFYING CROSS-TABULATION TABLES

One problem with cross-tabulation tables is that they can become large and unwieldy when the variables have many categories. The relationships contained in the table may be obscured by the large amount of detail provided. Furthermore, the Chi-Square test statistic may be inaccurate when there are a large number of cells in the table with frequencies smaller than five (see your textbook for a discussion of this point). A solution is to combine the categories of the variables into groupings of the original categories. Usually, when a strong relationship is apparent in a large cross-tabulation table, it will be equally apparent in a compressed table.

For instance, in the cross-tabulation table presented earlier, we might create two groups of variable A15 (Which dry cleaners do you use most often?) by combining Comet, One Hour and Other into a single category. Furthermore we might create two groups of A16 (Distance from Apex) by combining "Less than one mile" and "One to less than two miles" into one category and "Two to less than three miles," "Three to less than five miles" and "Five miles or greater" into another. The following **PROC** statements would do this and produce a cross-tabulation table:

```
IF (A16 EQ 1 OR A16 EQ 2) THEN DIST = 1;
IF (A16 EQ 3 OR A16 EQ 4 OR A16 EQ 5) THEN DIST = 2;
IF (A15 EQ 1) THEN  MOST = 1;
IF (A15 NE 1) THEN MOST = 2;
PROC FREQ DATA=CLEANERS;
     FORMAT MOST NEWMOST. DIST NEWDIST.;
     TABLES DIST*MOST/CHISQ NOPERCENT NOCOL;
```

SPSS Procedure - Place after the **DATA LIST** but before the **VALUE LABELS** statement:

```
IF (A16 EQ 1 OR A16 EQ 2) DIST = 1
IF (A16 EQ 3 OR A16 EQ 4 OR A16 EQ 5) DIST = 2
IF (A15 EQ 1) MOST = 1
IF (A15 NE 1) MOST = 2
```

Place the following statement just after the **END DATA** statement:

```
CROSSTABS TABLES = DIST BY MOST
STATISTICS 1
OPTIONS 2 3
```

```
                    TABLE OF DIST BY MOST

        DIST (HOW FAR IS APEX FROM YOUR HOME?)  BY
              MOST (WHICH DRY CLEANERS DO YOU USE MOST OFTEN?)

        FREQUENCY       |
        ROW PCT         |APEX    |OTHER   | TOTAL
        ----------------+--------+--------+
        < 2 MILES       |   37   |   32   |   69
                        | 53.62  | 46.38  |
        ----------------+--------+--------+
        2 OR MORE MILES |   26   |   86   |  112
                        | 23.21  | 76.79  |
        ----------------+--------+--------+
        TOTAL              63       118      181

                   FREQUENCY MISSING = 9

             STATISTICS FOR TABLE OF DIST BY MOST


        STATISTIC           DF     VALUE     PROB
        ------------------------------------------------
        CHI-SQUARE           1     17.399   0.000
```

We have converted variables A16 and A15 into two new variables named DIST and MOST by the **IF** statements, and each of the two new variables has two categories. The new variables will have missing values if the original variables were coded as missing, and, of course, these missing values do not appear in the table.

The relationship that was apparent in the original table continues to be apparent in the above table. Of those who live less than two miles from Apex, 53.62 percent say that they use Apex most often. Of those who live two or more miles from Apex, only 23.21 percent mention Apex as their first choice. The Chi-Square value is considerably smaller than in the twenty cell table. However, our new table has only one degree of freedom [(2 rows - 1) x (2 columns - 1)]. So although, the Chi-Square value is smaller, it continues to be highly significant. If the variables were independent, the likelihood of getting a Chi-Square value as large as 17.399 is less than one in ten thousand (values smaller than .0001 are indicated as .000).

Testing for Significant Differences. The condensed variables are also useful in calculating means for various groups with **PROC MEANS**. When calculating mean values, we will use the original four-category variable (A16X) as the numerical variable rather than the new variable (DIST), which has only two categories. This is because the original variable (A16X) contain a greater amount of mathematical detail.

```
PROC MEANS DATA=CLEANERS;
    VAR A16X;
PROC SORT DATA=CLEANERS;
    BY MOST;
PROC MEANS DATA=CLEANERS;
    BY MOST;
    VAR A16X;
```

```
SPSS Procedure - Place just after the END DATA statement:

    FREQUENCIES VARIABLES = A16X/
        STATISTICS MEAN STDDEV SEMEAN
    BREAKDOWN A16X BY MOST
```

The **PROC MEANS** above will produce statistics on variable A16 for each of the values of variable MOST as follows:

VARIABLE	N	MEAN	STANDARD DEVIATION	MINIMUM VALUE	MAXIMUM VALUE	STD ERROR OF MEAN	SUM	VARIANCE
A16X	191	2.549738	1.434128	.500000	6.000000	.103770	487.000000	2.056724

VARIABLE	N	MEAN	STANDARD DEVIATION	MINIMUM VALUE	MAXIMUM VALUE	STD ERROR OF MEAN	SUM	VARIANCE
------------------------------CLEANERS USED MOST OFTEN = . ---								
A16X	10	2.050000	1.065885	.500000	6.000000	.337062	20.500000	1.136111
-- MOST = 1 ---								
A16X	63	1.920635	1.329584	.500000	6.000000	.167518	121.000000	1.767793
-- MOST = 2 ---								
A16X	118	2.927966	1.391788	.500000	6.000000	.128125	345.500000	1.937075

The table above reveals that there were ten respondents who did not indicate a preferred dry cleaners. Those who use Apex most often live an average of 1.92 miles from Apex. Those who patronize other cleaners live an average of 2.93 miles from Apex. This appears to be a large difference. We might wonder if a similar large difference would occur if the another sample of similar size were taken using the same sampling procedures. Even if both customers and noncustomers lived the same average distance from Apex, we would expect some difference between our two estimates due to sampling error. If the difference were due to sampling error, we would not expect to find a large difference in repeated samples taken from the population. So, the important question for the analyst is, "How large a difference would convince us that customer and noncustomers live a different average distance from Apex?"

We may perform a simple test of the significance of this difference by using the following test statistic:

$$Z = \frac{\overline{x}_1 - \overline{x}_2}{\hat{s}_{\overline{x}_1 - \overline{x}_2}}$$

where:

$$\hat{s}_{\overline{x}_1 - \overline{x}_2} = \sqrt{\hat{s}_1^2 + \hat{s}_2^2}$$

$\overline{x}_1$ and $\overline{x}_2$ are the means for the two groups and $\hat{s}_1$ and $\hat{s}_2$ are the standard errors of the estimates of the mean. These may be taken directly from the **PROC MEANS** output. The pooled standard error is therefore calculated from the second equation above as:

$$\hat{s}_{\overline{x}_1 - \overline{x}_2} = \sqrt{.167518^2 + .128125^2} = .210894$$

Having calculated the pooled standard error, we may use the first equation to calculate the Z value for the difference between the means as:

$$Z = \frac{2.927966 - 1.920635}{.210894} = 4.776479$$

A table of the normal probability distribution indicates that the probability of getting a Z value as large as 4.78 is less than .001. This tells us that if the means are equal in the population, then there is a very small chance of getting a sample difference of the magnitude we are observing in our sample. We may reasonably conclude, based upon the differences in our sample means, that it is very unlikely that the true means are equal in these two groups of the population. This means that, for Apex Dry Cleaners, the distance people live from the establishment is a plausible motive for patronage.

CHOOSING CROSS-TABULATIONS AND MEAN BREAKDOWNS

Novice researchers often have difficulty in deciding what crosstabulations and/or mean breakdowns to perform. This occasionally leads students to cross-tabulate or break down "everything by everything." Obviously, in a data set with forty variables, such a complete cross-tabulation would generate 1600 cross-tabs. Besides the fact that half of these tables would be transpositions of the other half (A1 by A2 generates the same information as A2 by A1), it is unlikely that most researchers would perform a thorough analysis of 800 tables.

Another approach is to perform comparisons of all of the descriptive variables (e.g. Age,

Sex, Income, etc.) by the remaining variables in the data set. This should generate considerably fewer tables than the naive approach suggested above. And, although it may produce a large number of tables, the significance level of the Chi-Square statistic should help to focus attention on those tables in which the variables are likely to be related.

However, focusing on the descriptive variables may still cause the analyst to ignore important relationships among variables in the data set. For instance, in our example of a cross-tabulation, we observed a close relationship between the distance for Apex and use of Apex most often. Probably the most useful suggestion in choosing cross-tabulation is to focus on the objectives of the study and the hypotheses they imply. For instance, important objectives of the Apex study were to measure consumer brand preferences and to generate explanations for these preferences. The questions that we asked in our questionnaire imply that we may have several tentative explanations for these preferences. These explanations could include the amount spent on laundry and/or dry cleaning, the usage of coupons and specials, distance from Apex and the perceived attractiveness of service, specials, prices, location, and hours. Thus, the relationship between brand preference and each of these other variables should be explored.

A marketing research study may contain many different measures that follow from proposed marketing strategies. These measures should suggest ways of breaking down the sample. They might include:

1. respondents who are aware of a particular brand versus those who are not.
2. respondents who would consider the purchase a brand versus those who would not
3. respondents who have tried a particular brand versus those who haven't.
4. respondents who regular use a brand versus those who use other brands.
5. heavy users versus light users of a product category.
6. people who prefer to buy at different types of stores, such as grocery versus drug stores.

CONSTRUCTING SPLIT VARIABLES

Whether performing cross-tabulation or comparing the means between groups, it is necessary to define the groups. Sometimes this is quite easy. The analyst may actually be interested in inspecting a table containing all of the categories of the variables. This was illustrated in our five by four cross-tab containing twenty cells. Later, however, we summarized this table into a two-by-two table containing only four cells. This table is much more convenient for presenting the results of the research. In general, tables with only two (or, at the most, three) rows and or columns are easier to read and understand. Thus, a decision must sometimes be made as to how to reclassify the large number of categories into a smaller number. In the case of gender, there is no problem since there are only two categories. However, when variables have a larger number of categories, the decision may be more difficult. Of course, this decision cannot be made until the frequency distribution of each variable is observed and we can see how many respondents fall into each of the original groups.

Another reason for combining variables into a smaller number of categories has to do with statistical precision. Sampling theory suggests that the error in estimation of a parameter is related to the group size. In data sets such as the one you have gathered, a common problem is that the size of some groups may very small. Combining categories of variables can result in fewer categories with a larger number of observations in each. When combining, say, five categories into two, we would usually prefer to split the sample such that roughly half the respondents fall into each group. When this is not possible (sometimes it is not logical) we would still prefer that the smallest group contain at least one-third of the respondents.

CHOOSING THE APPROPRIATE ANALYSIS PROCEDURE - CROSS-TABULATION OR COMPARISON OF MEANS

We have discussed two different ways of investigating relationships among two or more variables in the data set; cross-tabulation and comparing mean values between groups (either directly or through t-tests). Students often experience confusion regarding which of these procedures to use. Because all of our data has been entered in the form of codes, each variable is, as a practical matter, categorical. Of course, some of the data may have ordinal quality and some ordinal variables may be transformed into "pseudo-interval data." Nevertheless, each variable is represented by a small number of coded categories. For this reason, it is nearly always acceptable, from a statistical point of view, to perform cross-tabulations.

Sometimes, when the data have numerical quality, it is desirable to compute additional summary statistics, such as the mean. This is not, however, appropriate when the data are inherently categorical in nature. For instance, the dry cleaners preferred most often is an inherently categorical variable. The number codes 1 through 4 serve only to identify one of the dry cleaning establishments. If we were to calculate the average value of this variable to be 1.963, this value would have no statistical meaning. This is because each of the four codes has not been used to specify a quantity but only to identify the response.

On the other hand, when the codes specify quantities, it may be appropriate to use **PROC MEANS** and t-tests. Further, even though it is acceptable to perform cross-tabulations on these types of variables, calculating mean values may be preferable because they summarize the data into a simpler form. Rather than presenting the percentages who chose each of several responses, the average combines all of these data into a single number.

As discussed in your textbook, interval and ratio data are the only types for which the calculation of a mean is strictly permissible. Other types of data, even though used to represent numerical quantities, will depart to a greater or lesser degree from the assumptions of interval-level measurement. "Pseudo-interval" data may depart slightly from these assumptions. The data generated from rating scales (such as the rating of the store attributes) may deviate even more. Nevertheless, average values for each of these types of data are commonly reported in commercial marketing research studies. When doing so, however, it is recommended that caveats be provided that the assumptions are being made regarding data quality and these assumptions may or may not be warranted.

CHAPTER NINE
THE RESEARCH REPORT

OVERVIEW OF THE RESEARCH REPORT

The research report (and presentation if required) will become the final product of your project efforts and may provide the major basis for the grade you receive. The comprehensiveness of your research report will depend upon the preferences of your instructor, just as commercial research reports will reflect the needs and desires of the client. Some clients will want little beyond the results, conclusions, and a thorough managerial summary. Others will expect a complete report, including a discussion of the background, research methodology, and results.

TITLE PAGE

The title page should include the following:

> The title of your project
> The course, section number and instructor
> The team identifier (e.g., Group 1, Team A)
> The names of the group members
> The client's name
> The date the project was completed

TABLE OF CONTENTS

The table of contents should list the major and minor headings of the research report and the pages upon which they appear. Next, you should include on a separate page a list of the tables contained in the report by table number, major title of the table, and the page on which it appears. Another section should follow, listing figures and/or exhibits in the same format as the listing of tables.

TABLE 9.1
OUTLINE OF THE RESEARCH REPORT

TITLE PAGE
TABLE OF CONTENTS
MANAGERIAL SUMMARY
BACKGROUND
OBJECTIVES
RESEARCH DESIGN AND METHODOLOGY
    Research Method
    Sampling
    Data Collection
    Tabulation and Analysis Procedures
RESULTS (Tables, Graphics, and Discussion)
    Annotated Questionnaire
    Description of the Sample
    Findings Keyed to Each Objective
CONCLUSIONS AND RECOMMENDATIONS
LIMITATIONS
APPENDICES

MANAGERIAL SUMMARY

The managerial summary is considered by many to be the most important part of the research report. There may be only a few people who will read the entire report in detail. Higher level managers will focus on the managerial summary and refer to the report itself only to seek additional detail.

The managerial summary should not try to summarize the entire report. Rather, it should hit each important high point, leaving the reader with a good understanding of what was done and what was found. When properly written, the managerial summary should be able to stand on its own as a brief but complete description of the project, its findings, conclusions, and recommendations. It should do this in a few pages.

Although the managerial summary will be included near the beginning of the report, it probably will not be written until the report is complete. After writing the report, you should carefully review it to extract the key points to be included in the summary. In one format of the managerial summary, numbered points will be presented, usually in the order they are contained in the report. Each of these points will be a sentence, or at the most two, summarizing some key aspect of the report. The numbered points might be divided into separate sections, such as Objectives and Methodology, Findings, and Conclusions and Recommendations. Some items that could be contained in the managerial summary include:

1.   **OBJECTIVES AND METHODOLOGY**
   a.   The general purpose of the study.
   b.   The type of research methodology used (e.g., primary versus secondary data, exploratory versus descriptive versus causal research, survey versus experiment).
   c.   How the sampling was conducted (the type of sample, its size, and a brief description of the methodology).
   d.   How and where the data was collected.

2.   **FINDINGS**
   This will often be the longest part of the managerial summary and will contain each key finding that is relevant to the research objectives. At least one such finding will be listed for each of the objectives originally specified in the research proposal. The findings explain what was learned from the study.

3.   **CONCLUSIONS AND RECOMMENDATIONS**
   The managerial summary should contain a brief statement of each conclusion and recommendation made. These generally follow from the findings that were presented in the previous section. Directions for future research can also be provided.

BACKGROUND

Describing the background of the study should be a fairly straightforward task if you have written a good research proposal. Much of what is contained in this section will be a paraphrase of the proposal, although it will be written in the past rather than future tense. The background discussion could include a brief summary of the client interview and any other information gathered from secondary sources, such as a literature review or the results of previous studies of a similar nature.

OBJECTIVES

In this section, you should briefly describe the motivation for conducting the study and provide a general statement of its purpose. Specific managerial decisions that will be supported by the survey should be described in as much detail as possible. Finally, the specific research objectives to be accomplished should be listed and discussed.

RESEARCH DESIGN AND METHODOLOGY

Most of the decisions regarding research methodology will have been presented in the original research proposal.   However, your actual study may have required some modifications of these plans. Thus, this section should discuss the original research design, as well as any necessary deviations.

Research Methodology. First, the type of research methodology used should be discussed. Clearly, your study has relied upon primary data. However, you might want to discuss why this type of data is particularly appropriate to your research objectives. In addition, your study is a descriptive research study, and you should describe why this type of research method was appropriate in accomplishing your research objectives. One of your key decisions was to specify what type of data-gathering method would be used (e.g., intercept interview, telephone interview, or self-administered questionnaire). You should present the rationale for how this choice was made, paying attention to both the advantages and disadvantages of each method. Focus on how the chosen methodology was appropriate to the accomplishment of the research objectives.

Sampling. You should discuss the type of sampling method you chose and the rationale for this choice. You should further explain how the research objectives are most likely to be accomplished by the chosen sampling method. Next, you should carefully describe and discuss the specific methods you used to select your sample. Any difficulties encountered in specifying and selecting the sample should be mentioned, especially as they might affect the quality of the results. Finally, present a brief discussion of how the sample size was chosen and a statement about the expected precision of the survey.

Data Collection. In this section, you should describe how, when, and where the data was actually gathered. Particular attention should be paid to problems encountered in the field, such as respondent cooperativeness, nonresponse, difficulties in respondents understanding the questionnaire, and any other aspects of data collection that might have affected the quality of the results.

Tabulation and Analysis. The tabulation and analysis section should contain a brief summary of:

1. the procedures used for screening the questionnaires for accuracy and completeness.
2. the procedures used to code open-ended questions.
3. information about data record layout and how data entry was performed.
4. a description of the hardware and software programs used for tabulation and analysis.
5. a description of the software procedures used for tabulation and analysis.

RESULTS

Annotated Questionnaire. Usually, the first few runs of your SAS program will include a **PROC FREQ** for all the variables in the data set and a **PROC MEANS** for all of the numerical variables. This will generate at least as many tables as there are variables in the data set. You will probably not want to use all of the data from these tables in the main body of the report. Only those that focus on the objectives and enhance the readers' understanding of the results need be included.

However, your client will probably want to have a convenient method of viewing the general results of the entire survey. One means of doing this is to present the client with a complete set of computer printouts. (Your instructor may or may not request this as a part of the materials you turn in. If printouts are turned in, they are normally bound together as a separate item from the report itself.) However, computer printouts are cumbersome and require some effort in extracting the data. Your job as an analyst is to make the results as clear as possible to the client.

A more convenient method of presenting the results of the survey is to prepare an annotated questionnaire. It would normally be included as an appendix to your report and a discussion of it will be presented at the beginning of the "Results" section.

Preparing the annotated questionnaire is a simple matter of extracting key figures from the computer printouts and placing them on a clean copy of the questionnaire you used in the study. For instance, recall our question, "How far do you live from Apex?" It would appear as follows on our annotated questionnaire:

9.   **Approximately how far is Apex Dry Cleaners from your home? (PLACE RESPONSE INTO ONE OF THE FOLLOWING CATEGORIES)**

                                                                          (21)
LESS THAN ONE MILE 12.0%
ONE MILE OR MORE BUT LESS THAN TWO MILES 26.2%
TWO MILES OR MORE BUT LESS THAN THREE MILES 34.0%
THREE MILES OR MORE BUT LESS THAN FIVE MILES 20.9%
FIVE MILES OR MORE 6.8%
REFUSED OR DON'T KNOW . . . . 9 missing responses
          Average distance =   2.55 miles

It is especially easy to prepare the annotated questionnaire if you have used a word processor in constructing it. All you have to do is delete the answer codes for the questions and insert the results taken from the printout. If you have not used a word processor, you might use a clean copy of the questionnaire, delete the original codes with copy correction fluid, and insert the values from the printout.

You must decide how much information to place on the annotated questionnaire. For most questions that have categorical responses, you will present the percentage of the nonmissing values falling into each category. These percentages are usually of greater interest than the actual frequency counts. When the data have numerical quality, as in the example above, it may be more useful to provide some type of summary measure, usually the average value. Sometimes, this average value may be all that is needed to represent the responses of such questions as attitude scales. For example here is an annotated portion of the rating scale section of our Apex questionnaire:

ITEM	RATING SCALES: 1 = EXCELLENT 2 = GOOD 3 = FAIR 4 = POOR			IMPORTANCE: 1=EXTREMELY 2=VERY 3=SOMEWHAT 4=NOT
	APEX	**COMET**	**ONE HOUR**	**IMPORTANCE**
Customer Service	1.84	2.09	1.93	1.88
Hours	2.25	2.25	1.65	1.87
Prices	2.18	1.76	2.04	1.95
Location	2.00	2.00	1.82	1.45
Specials	2.21	2.01	1.81	1.84

Composition of the Sample. The first part of the results section will usually contain a description of the composition of the sample, which may be accompanied by a summary table of key descriptive characteristics. This will help familiarize the reader with the respondents from whom the data has been gathered. It is not necessary to present all of the data you included in the annotated questionnaire. For instance, in Table 9.2, the categorical frequencies have been reduced to percentages or averages for the entire sample.

You could present a brief discussion of Table 9.2 pointing out that the description of the sample is consistent with what is believed about the population based upon the researcher's experience or, perhaps by comparison with known census data.

When the data are numerical (e.g., age, or income), the average is a useful summary measure. However, when the data are categorical (e.g., sex or occupation), each category should be presented, along with its percentage. One way of supporting the presentation of categorical data is to construct pie charts indicating the percentage of the respondents falling into each category.

TABLE 9.2
COMPOSITION OF THE SAMPLE

CHARACTERISTIC	SUBGROUP	VALUE
AVERAGE AGE		42.3
AVERAGE FAMILY INCOME		$42,166
SEX	MALE	32 %
	FEMALE	68 %
MARITAL STATUS	MARRIED	67 %
	SINGLE	33 %
FAMILY SIZE (Married only)		2.43
TYPE RESIDENCE	SINGLE-FAMILY HOME	62 %
	APARTMENT, DUPLEX	44 %
	CONDOMINIUM	4 %
OCCUPATION	PROFESSIONAL	10 %
	PROPRIETOR, MANAGER	17 %
	CLERICAL, SALES, SKILLED	24 %
	BLUE-COLLAR	21 %
	STUDENT	21 %
	OTHER	7 %

Graphics, such as the pie chart of Figure 9.1, can be used to enhance the appearance of the report and may increase the clarity of the presentation. Graphics are especially effective visual aids when making an oral report.

Findings. The next part of the results section presents your research findings keyed to the project objectives. The basis for your findings will be one or more tables constructed from the computer output. The tables you use in your report will usually provide less detail than the computer output. In constructing tables, your goal should be to use the simplest table

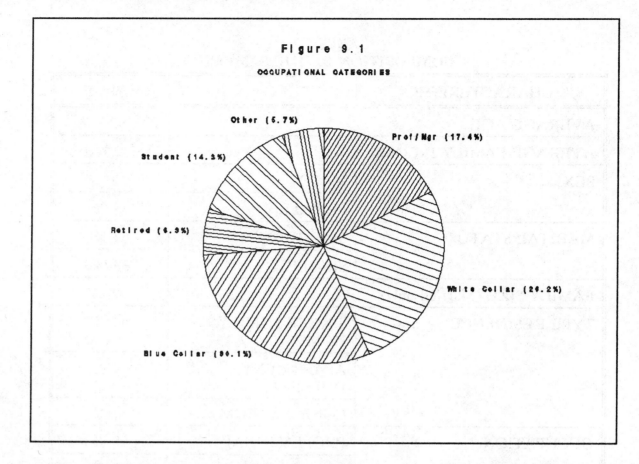

Figure 9.1

OCCUPATIONAL CATEGORIES

Other (5.7%)

Prof/Mgr (17.4%)

Student (14.5%)

White Collar (24.2%)

Retired (4.9%)

Blue Collar (56.1%)

that will support the finding you are presenting. For example, the output from **PROC FREQ** may have included both frequencies and percentages for each cell. Perhaps presenting only the percentages will support the finding just as well. In addition, you may want to compress your cross class-tabulation tables into two-by-two or, at the most, three-by-three tables. It is much easier to see relationships in smaller tables and, if the relationship is statistically significant it will usually show up just as clearly, if not more clearly, in a collapsed table. Condensing cross-tabulation tables by combining the categories of variables was discussed in Chapters Seven and Eight.

Order of Presentation of Findings. The analyst must decide on the order of presentation of the results so that the report flows in a clear and logical manner. One way to present the results is to follow the order presented within the questionnaire. In small surveys or surveys that focus on one specific area, such as pricing, this may be a satisfactory method. However, when the researcher has specified clear research objectives, it is more logical to divide the results of the study into sections that focus on one or a few specific objectives. When the report is written in this manner, all the data contained in the questionnaire that relates to the specific objective will be pulled together around a single unifying theme. This allows for a more coherent discussion and provides stronger support for conclusions. In discussing how the findings may be presented, let us suppose that two of our research objectives were as follows:

1.   **To develop a descriptive profile of Apex customers versus noncustomers.**

2.   **To determine the importance of various product/service attributes in choosing a dry cleaning establishment.**

Analysis of Subgroups. The first objective would involve a comparison of customers versus noncustomers on a variety of different descriptive and attitudinal measures. The first table we might present would be a set of averages or percentages taken from the **PROC MEANS** and **PROC FREQ** output. Note that the categories of Table 9.3 are similar to those in Table 9.2. However, when a categorical variable has only two categories (e.g., male versus female), only the percentages for one of the categories are presented. The percentage for the other category will be obvious since the two must add to one hundred percent.

Table 9.3 suggests some interesting differences between Apex customers and noncustomers. Apex customers appear to be younger, are less likely to be married, are less likely to live in single-family homes, and have lower average incomes than noncustomers. Apex customers are also more likely to be students and to live considerably closer to Apex than noncustomers. All these differences are statistically significant at the .02 level. This tells us that if the means or proportions were equal in the population, the chance of getting sampling differences of these magnitudes is less than two in one hundred. The method of testing for differences in means and proportions discussed in Chapter Seven (t-tests) was used to perform these tests.

TABLE 9.3
SAMPLE CHARACTERISTICS BROKEN DOWN BY
PATRONAGE OF APEX VERSUS OTHER

ITEM	TOTAL n = 200	PREFERRED DRY CLEANERS		*Sig. p <
		APEX n = 44	OTHER n = 168	
AVERAGE AGE	42.3	34.4	46.6	.01
% MALE	32 %	37 %	30 %	n.s.
% MARRIED	67 %	48 %	76 %	.01
% SINGLE-FAMILY HOMES	62 %	21 %	77 %	.01
% Students	22 %	32 %	16 %	.02
AVERAGE INCOME	$ 42,167	$ 32,667	$ 46,595	.01
MILES FROM APEX	2.58	1.92	2.93	.01

*Only differences that are significant with p < .10 are reported

Presentation of Rating Scales. We next construct a table of the average ratings of Apex versus the average ratings of its primary competitors to obtain an idea about customer attitudes toward patronage characteristics. This table (Table 9.4) also presents the average importance score for each of the characteristics.

TABLE 9.4
PATRONAGE ATTRIBUTES
AVERAGE RATINGS AND IMPORTANCES
FOR EACH ESTABLISHMENT

ITEM	AVERAGE RATINGS n = 181			IMPORT-ANCE n = 181
	APEX	COMET	ONE-HOUR	
Customer Service	1.84	2.09	1.94	1.88
Hours	2.26	2.25	1.66	1.89
Prices	2.19	1.76	2.03	1.96
Location	1.98	1.99	1.85	1.46
Specials	2.23	1.99	1.81	1.82

RATING SCALE:
1 = Excellent
2 = Good
3 = Fair
4 = Poor

IMPORTANCE SCALE
1 = Extremely Important
2 = Very Important
3 = Somewhat Important
4 = Not Important

Several interesting things may be noted from Table 9.4:

1. Respondents reported that the most important characteristic in choosing a dry cleaners is location, with an average importance of 1.46 (roughly between extremely important and very important). Apex's rating on this characteristic (1.98) is below One Hour, which does well with an average rating of 1.85, and barely above Comet which is rated worst, with an average 1.99 rating.
2. Clearly, with regard to important characteristics in choosing a dry cleaners, location is a dominant characteristics. Each of the other factors is roughly one-half rating point lower in importance.
3. Although price is rated as the least important patronage characteristic, Apex has the poorest average rating on this characteristic. Of slightly greater importance is "Specials," another characteristic on which Apex does relatively poorly.
4. Apex's most positive characteristic is its customer service, a moderately important characteristic on which it does better than One Hour and much better than Comet.
5. Apex and Comet are also rated worst on hours, an area in which One Hour is clearly doing very well.

Breakdown of Rating Scales. The above findings suggest that Apex is not doing very well on three fairly important patronage characteristics, price, specials and hours. However, keep in mind that the ratings and importance scores in Table 9.4 are average values computed across the entire sample. We might wonder if both customers and noncustomers view Apex in the same way. We could run **PROC MEANS** for the scaled ratings of Apex broken down by preferred dry cleaners and construct Table 9.5:

TABLE 9.5
AVERAGE RATINGS OF APEX
BROKEN DOWN BY PREFERRED DRY CLEANERS

ITEM	TOTAL SAMPLE n = 181	PREFERRED DRY CLEANERS		*Sig. p <
		APEX n = 65	OTHER n = 126	
CUSTOMER SERVICE	1.84	1.60	1.97	.01
HOURS	2.26	2.10	2.34	.07
PRICES	2.19	2.08	2.25	n.s.
LOCATION	1.98	1.65	2.15	.01
SPECIALS	2.23	2.08	2.30	.10

*Only differences that are significant with $p < .10$ are reported.

Clearly, on all patronage characteristics, Apex is doing much better among its own customers than among regular customers of other establishments.   On all characteristics except price, the differences are statistically significant with a probability of less than .10. Table 9.5 supports the tentative conclusion that location is very important. This table tells us that, although Apex is rated relatively low on location by the total sample, it is rated more highly by its own customers, and this difference is statistically significant at the .01 level. Apex customers are also very pleased with the quality of customer service they receive ($p < .01$). Location and, to some extent, customer service may be important patronage motives for Apex customers because noncustomers rate Apex much lower in both of these areas. Although its own customers rate Apex higher in the areas of hours, prices and specials, customer satisfaction in these areas is much lower than in the areas of location and service.

Presenting Rating Scales as Graphics. When presenting rating scale data, the clarity of the presentation may be improved through the use of graphics. The bar chart of Figure 9.2 presents the essential characteristics of the data contained in Table 9.5. Note that in order to present the values, it is useful to reverse the direction of the scale such that taller bars indicate more positive ratings. This is done by subtracting each rating from 4.0, such that a rating of 3.0 corresponds with an "excellent" rating and 0.0 corresponds with a rating of "poor."

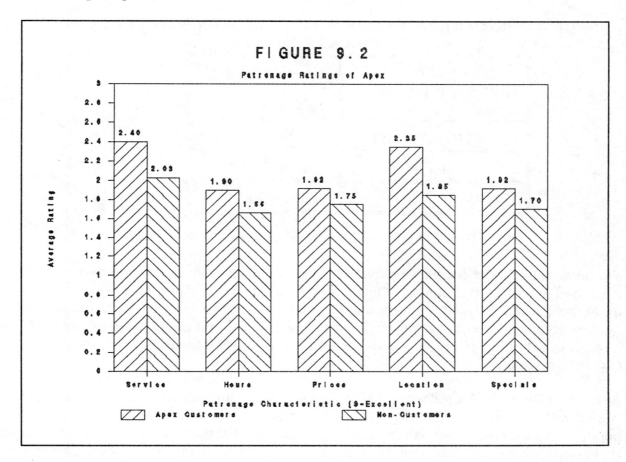

Cross-Tabulation. We might further investigate the importance of location by presenting the following cross class-tabulation table:

TABLE 9.6
PERCENTAGE CHOOSING APEX BROKEN DOWN BY
DISTANCE FROM APEX

DISTANCE FROM APEX	Percent Choosing		% OF SAMPLE
	APEX	OTHER	
LESS THAN 2 MILES	53.6 %	46.4 %	38.1 %
2 OR MORE MILES	23.2 %	76.8 %	61.9 %
TOTAL	34.8 %	65.2 %	100.0 %

CHI-SQUARE = 17.4   SIGNIFICANCE = < .001

We note that of those people who live less than two miles from Apex, 53.6 percent choose it as their favorite dry cleaners. On the other hand, among those who live two or more miles from Apex, only 23.2 percent make it their first choice. Furthermore the high Chi-Square value and the very small significance level suggest that this finding did not occur as a result of sampling error. There is only one chance in one thousand that this difference occurred by chance.

Additional Detail in Breakdowns. The previous analysis suggests a conclusion that location is a powerful motive for choosing Apex as the most preferred dry cleaners. However, it is possible that location is only an important precondition for patronage. This is apparent in that approximately forty-six percent of those who live less than two miles from Apex still do not patronize it regularly. There are probably other reasons for not choosing Apex. Later in our report we would want to discuss strategies for attracting new customers from this group.

PROC MEANS allows you to compute the value of variables for combinations of values of other variables. For example:

```
PROC MEANS;
    VAR A16 A17--A21 A37--A42;
    BY DIST MOST;
```

The **PROC MEANS** presented above will calculate the means of the numerical questions for each combination of the two values of the variables DIST and MOST (the two-category variables created in Chapter Eight). Thus, four sets of numerical statistics will be calculated for variables A16, A17 TO A21 and A37 to A42. The four sets of statistics will be for the following groups:

Apex customers	Live less than two miles from Apex
Apex customers	Live two or more miles from Apex
Apex noncustomers	Live less than two miles from Apex
Apex noncustomers	Live two or more miles from Apex

We could select from the output the values for noncustomers who live less than two miles from Apex and compare them with the values for all Apex customers. Table 9.7 presents the average values for the total sample along with the values for these two groups. We see that, on most descriptive characteristics, non-customers who live close to Apex still differ significantly from Apex customers. Although they are only slightly older (difference not significant), they are more likely to be married, have higher average incomes, and are more likely to live in single family homes. Although the table indicates that non-customers live closer to Apex, this is an artifact of the way the two groups were defined. The first group contains all Apex customers, regardless of their distance from Apex while the second group only includes non-customers who live within two miles of Apex.

The lower part of Table 9.7 reveals that noncustomers who live near Apex also differ regard to their perceptions of Apex. Apex's own customers rate them higher in every area and the difference is statistically significant with regard to location. Perhaps, regarding location, Apex customers find it more convenient to get to and from the store. Others, who also live a short distance from the store may not find the traffic patterns as convenient. The fact that most of the ratings are not statistically significant is most likely due to the small size of the sample of non-customers who live within two miles.

TABLE 9.7
CHARACTERISTICS AND RATINGS OF APEX BY
APEX CUSTOMERS VERSUS
NON-CUSTOMERS WHO LIVE WITHIN TWO MILES OF APEX

ITEM	TOTAL SAMPLE n = 200	APEX CUSTOMERS n = 61	NON-CUSTOMERS WITHIN 2 MILES n = 34	Sig. p <
AVERAGE AGE	42.5	34.4	37.8	n.s.
% MALE	32 %	37 %	25 %	n.s.
% MARRIED	66 %	48 %	74 %	.01
% SINGLE-FAMILY HOMES	62 %	24 %	56 %	.01
AVERAGE INCOME	$ 42,167	$ 32,667	$ 45,726	.05
DISTANCE FROM APEX	2.58	1.92	1.34	.01
AVERAGE RATINGS				
Customer Service	1.84	1.60	1.78	n.s.
Hours	2.26	2.10	2.35	n.s.
Prices	2.19	2.08	2.29	n.s.
Location	1.98	1.65	2.03	.06
Specials	2.23	2.08	2.33	n.s.

CONCLUSIONS AND RECOMMENDATIONS

This section is usually the most important part of the research report. It tells the client what the results mean and what the research group thinks should be done. Conclusions and recommendations are not the same. A conclusion is a statement of what the analyst believes the findings mean. A recommendation suggests a course of action that should be pursued.

The following conclusions would be suggested by the analysis presented in the previous section:

1. Apex customers differ from noncustomers in significant ways. The typical Apex customer is younger, has a lower annual family income, is more likely to be single, and is less likely to live in a single family home.

2. The typical Apex customer lives less than two miles from Apex. Of the respondents who live three or more miles from Apex, only twenty-three percent make Apex their preferred choice.

3. The most important patronage motive in choosing a dry cleaners is location. All other characteristics are somewhat less important. Surprisingly, price is the least important patronage motive to members of the overall sample.

4. Of the three dry cleaning establishments rated by members of the sample, Apex is rated first only on customer service. One-Hour is perceived to have the best overall hours, while Comet leads in the areas of prices and specials.

5. Apex is perceived much more positively by its own customers than by customers of other establishments. On the most important characteristic of location, Apex gets high overall ratings from its own customers. This is not surprising, since the average Apex customer lives 1.92 miles from Apex while the average noncustomer lives 2.93 miles away.

6. On characteristics other than location, Apex customers give Apex higher ratings than do noncustomers. Thus, the lower ratings assigned by noncustomers may stem from a lack of direct experience in dealing with Apex.

7. Although Apex receives high ratings from its own customers on customer service, its customers do not appear to be especially satisfied with its hours of operation or its prices. It is possible that Apex customer service is better than it needs to be to satisfy current customers and that some customers would make trade-offs of better hours and lower prices for a slightly lower level of customer service.

8. Although location appears extremely important in choosing a dry cleaners, forty six percent of those who live less than two miles from Apex do not patronize it. This forty-six percent may represent a seriously under-exploited marketing opportunity. These close-in non-customers appear to differ significantly from regular Apex customers in terms of descriptive characteristics as well as in their attitudes toward Apex regarding important patronage motives.

The conclusions above would support the following recommendations:

1. Further research should be conducted among current customers to explore the trade-off between customer service, prices, hours, and specials. It may be that some customers are willing to sacrifice some aspects of customer service in favor of other patronage characteristics. However, no such trade-offs should be made until further research is conducted.

2. This study supports the conclusion that location is a vital patronage motive. Thus, any future location decisions must be made very carefully. A new location for Apex may also imply a very different target market from the one that is currently being satisfied, perhaps resembling the regular customers of competitors. Thus, a new location may require a different style of operation tailored to a different type of customer.

3. There appears to be a seriously under-exploited market opportunity among potential customers who live near Apex. These prospective customers exhibit descriptive characteristics different from Apex customers. They also differ in their attitudes about Apex's hours, prices, specials, and customer service. Thus, a promotional campaign should be targeted to this group through discounts and specials to encourage them to try Apex. Coupons and specials that would have a differential appeal to younger, non-married, less affluent consumers would be most effective.

LIMITATIONS

One of the most important things you will learn in your study of marketing research concerns its limitations. Nearly all marketing research studies have inherent limitations. Some of the limitations will be apparent to the client and others you have a responsibility to point out. Throughout this project manual (as well as throughout your marketing research textbook), you have been exposed to a variety of these limitations. In this section of the research report, you should highlight some of the key limitations of your project, such as:

1. The project is limited in scope due to restrictions on the length of the questionnaire.

2. The objectives of the questionnaire are limited by the type of project. Predictions about the outcome of marketing actions are the province of experimental research, not descriptive research.

3. The size of the sample restricts the accuracy of the results.

4. The definition of the population may be restricted due to resource constraints or the availability of adequate sampling frames. Thus, the results can only be generalized with confidence to the group from whom the sample was taken.

5. Many types of nonsampling errors may affect the quality of the data, including noncontact, nonresponse, interviewer bias in selecting respondents, and poor questionnaire design.

APPENDICES

Often, you will want to include information in your report that is not deemed sufficiently important to put in the main body. This information may be included in the appendices. Some typical items found in appendices are:

1. A copy of your screening questionnaire (if used).
2. A copy of the annotated questionnaire.
3. Information related to sampling, such as maps marked with the locations where interviewing took place.
4. A listing of the computer program and raw input data.
5. Technical information, such as formulas and procedures for determining sample sizes, confidence intervals, and difference testing.
6. Copies of any forms you might have prepared for a special purpose (e.g., call record sheets or coding forms).

ORAL REPORTS

Oral reports have a lot in common with the managerial summary: the limited time available forces the researcher to focus on key findings, conclusions, and recommendations. It is unlikely that the members of the audience will have a great interest in the background and methodology of the research. If they do, they should know that these details are provided in the full report. Often, people attend an oral presentation who are simply not interested in reading the report. They may want to know little more than what was learned and what it means.

It is important to avoid technical jargon in oral reports although you may need to know such things as the statistical significance of the results in case someone asks; however, normally statistical significance is not included as a main point of discussion.

You will want to develop an outline for the oral report audience. The purpose of the outline is to provide the audience with an overview of what you are going to talk about, not to summarize it. You may want to distribute a copy of the managerial summary after you have delivered the presentation. During the presentation, it is best to keep the audience's attention focused on the presenter.

Most of the findings and conclusions given during the oral report will be supported by either graphics or *simple* tables. These should be prepared in advance by creating transparencies (occasionally, color slides are used). It is unlikely that you will present all the tables or figures that you used to support a particular conclusion in the written report. The simplest way to make your point will usually be the best way. For instance, earlier we provided several tables to provide strong support for the conclusion that location was a vitally important factor in choosing a dry cleaners. In our oral report, we might use Table 9.6 alone or even a simplified version of it.

If your instructor requests that your group present its findings to the class, your presentation should probably include:

1.   A brief discussion of the background of the project, the client, the client's information needs, and the project objectives.

2.   A brief discussion of the research methodology chosen, the sampling method, and the sample size.

3.   Key findings and conclusions.

4.   Recommendations to the client.

5.   Any special problems you encountered that might be of interest to the other members of the class.

6.   Anything else the instructor requests.

CHAPTER TEN
MULTIVARIATE ANALYSIS

Chapters Eight and Nine focused on tabulation, crosstabulation, and the computation of basic statistical summary measures. A number of other useful multivariate analysis methods are discussed in your marketing research textbook. The purpose of multivariate analysis is to explore the simultaneous relationships among several variables. A discussion of these methods and how the output is analyzed is outside the scope of this project manual. However, in this chapter, we will provide a brief overview of some of these techniques, along with a typical SAS job set-up to run them. In most cases, the job setups describe the simplest usage of each procedure and will use the default values incorporated in the procedure. You should consult the SAS or SPSS manual for a complete discussion of the variety of options regarding statistics, output, and analysis methods.

REGRESSION ANALYSIS

The most commonly used multivariate technique is regression analysis. A regression equation develops a relationship between a dependent variable and one or more predictor variables. The dependent variable in a regression analysis should almost always be a numerical variable, although in special cases, it may be a dummy variable (a variable that has only two values, zero and one). The predictor variables must be either numerical or dummy variables.

In the Apex Dry Cleaning example, we might have attempted to predict the monthly dollar amount spent on dry cleaning as a function of the importance placed on various aspects of patronage and descriptive measures (e.g., age, sex, income, and distance from Apex).

The following SAS **PROC** statement provides an example of a typical regression analysis job set-up.

```
PROC REG DATA = CLEANERS;
    MODEL SPENDTOT=A13 A37 A38X A39 A40 A42X;
```

SPSS Procedure:

    REGRESSION   **VARIABLES** = SPENDTOT A13 A37 A38X
    A39 A40 A42X/
    DEPENDENT = SPENDTOT/STEPWISE

In the SAS **PROC** statement listed above, the variable SPENDTOT is the dependent variable, and the variables A13, A37, A38X, A39, A40, and A42X are the predictor variables. You will normally report the regression results as an equation of the form:

$$Y = \alpha + \beta_1 X_1 + \beta_2 X_2 + \ldots + \beta_n X_n$$

where α is the intercept term and β_1, β_2,...,β_n are the slope coefficients taken from the regression output.

Regression allows many options for specifying the model and there are a variety of problems (e.g., multicollinearity) that you may have to deal with. Your textbook discusses these issues, and the SAS statistics manual provides many additional programming options that may be specified. At a minimum in your analysis, you will want to report:

1.   The regression equation.

2.   The order of entry of the variables if the stepwise option has been selected.

3.   The interpretation of the slope and intercept coefficients.

4.   The results of significance testing of the slope and intercept coefficients.

5.   The proportion of the variation in the dependent variable that is explained by the predictor variables (the R^2).

DISCRIMINANT ANALYSIS

Discriminant analysis is an especially appropriate technique for market segmentation studies. This technique develops a relationship between a set of predictor variables (similar to the types of variables used in regression) and membership in a group (e.g., buyers versus nonbuyers, those who watch a particular television program versus those who do not). Cross-tabulations or tests of differences between the means are the most common ways to explore the relationship between membership in a group and some other categorical (e.g., sex) or numerical variable (e.g., income). Discriminant analysis, on the other hand, uses *several* predictor variables simultaneously (e.g. male/female, age, income, and distance from Apex) to predict the group of which each person is a member. In our Apex example, we might use "prefers Apex/does not prefer Apex" as the grouping variable. Thus, discriminant analysis recognizes that a *collection* of variables might be a better predictor of group membership than any single predictor alone.

A discriminant analysis equation resembles a regression equation in that the predictor variables are numerical or dummy variables. However, discriminant analysis attempts to find a linear combination of the predictor variables such that this linear combination is related, as closely as possible, to membership or nonmembership in the group. The computed value of this linear combination is sometimes referred to as a Z score (or discriminant score) for each respondent.

$$Z = \beta_1 X_1 + \beta_2 X_2 + \ldots + \beta_n X_n$$

The following SAS **PROC** statement would perform a discriminant analysis on our data set from Chapters Eight and Nine:

```
PROC DISCRIM DATA=CLEANERS PCORR LIST;
    CLASS MOST;
    VAR A17--A21;
```

```
SPSS Procedure:

    DISCRIMINANT GROUPS = MOST(1,2)/
        VARIABLES = A17 TO A21/
        ANALYSIS = A17 TO A21/
        METHOD = WILKS
```

The grouping variable need not be a dummy variable (having two categories) but could be a variable composed of several groups (e.g., respondents who patronize Apex, Comet, One-Hour, or Other). However, as the number of groups increases beyond two, additional difficulties in interpretation of the results are likely to be encountered.

In regression analysis, the R^2 value is important in indicating the closeness of the relationship between the predictor variables and the dependent variable. In discriminant analysis, one indication of the closeness of the relationship is the hit-miss table that shows the percentage of the members of the groups who are correctly classified. For example, suppose that of 181 respondents with non-missing values, 100 of them were known to prefer Apex as their favorite dry cleaners. It may be that the discriminant equation is capable of classifying only 92 of them correctly as preferring Apex. The other eight are misclassified as preferring some other cleaners. This would mean that the set of descriptive characteristics used as predictors in the discriminant analysis can be used to identify Apex customers with an accuracy of 92 percent.

If the number of respondents is sufficient, the discriminant scoring equation should be calibrated on one group of respondents and then be used to classify a second group of respondents, referred to as a holdout sample. Reclassifying the original respondents may result in an overstatement of the quality of the discriminant analysis results. SAS provides an option for doing this.

CLUSTER ANALYSIS

Cluster analysis is a method for identifying groups of respondents with similar patterns of response on several variables. A typical application of cluster analysis is in identifying benefit segments. These segments are groups of consumers who assign similar levels of importance to product features. Earlier, we asked the respondents how important each of the five patronage attributes were in selecting a dry cleaners. Suppose that one group (cluster) of respondents assigned a high level of importance to price and location and relatively low importance to the other three characteristics. Another group of consumers assigned low importance to price and location but high levels of importance to the other characteristics. A cluster analysis will analyze the patterns of responses to these five questions and assign respondents to groups such that:

1.   all members of each group have similar response patterns and

2.   each group has different response patterns from the other groups.

The following SAS **PROC** statements would form two clusters of respondents, create a variable identifying the membership of each respondent, and print out the means of each group for the five variables of interest:

```
PROC FASTCLUS DATA=CLEANERS OUT=CLUSOUT MAXC=2 LIST;
     VAR A32--A36;
PROC SORT DATA=CLUSOUT;
     BY CLUSTER;
PROC FREQ DATA=CLUSOUT;
     TABLES CLUSTER*A37--A42/NOCOL NOPERCENT CHISQ;
```

```
SPSS Procedure:

     QUICK CLUSTER A32 TO A36
          /CRITERIA=CLUSTER(2)
          /PRINT=CLUSTER
          /SAVE=CLUSTER(CLUSMEM)
     CROSSTABS TABLES=CLUSMEM BY A37 TO A42
     STATISTICS 1
     OPTIONS 3
```

The **PROC FASTCLUS** statement causes the program to perform a cluster analysis of the data allowing a maximum of two clusters (you may specify any number of clusters as long as it is less than the number of respondents). The output will provide a listing of the original respondents along with an identification of the cluster to which each is assigned. The procedure also creates a new SAS data set (to which we have given the name CLUSOUT). This new data set contains all of the original variables plus two additional variables named CLUSTER and DISTANCE. These two variables are automatically generated by the program and are added to the old data set. Additional SAS **PROC** statements (such as **MEANS** and **FREQ**) may be run using the new SAS data set CLUSOUT as the input data set, and the new variables CLUSTER and DISTANCE may be used in the same ways as those variables that were input or created by a variable transformation. This is illustrated in the second part of the above **PROC** statement. Had we believed that the cluster analysis was useful in identifying two market segments (we could call them benefit segments), **PROC FREQ** and **PROC MEANS** would help us further describe them using other variables in the data set such as the descriptive characteristics.

FACTOR ANALYSIS

Whereas cluster analysis attempts to identify groupings of respondents with similar response patterns, factor analysis attempts to find groupings of *variables* that appear to be related to each other. Consider our Apex Dry Cleaners example. It is possible that most people who assigned a positive rating to the price variable also assigned a positive rating to the specials variable. Likewise, when a positive rating was assigned to customer service, a similar high rating may have been assigned to hours. Thus, of our five rating scale variables, it is possible that there are, in fact, three groups of variables:

> Price and specials
> Customer service and hours
> Location

Factor analysis combines the original variables into linear composites called factor scores. This is analogous to calculating the average value of a number of variables. However, when calculating an average, equal weight is given to each value included in the calculation. A factor score is a *weighted* composite, and each variable is allowed to have a different weight such that all do not contribute equally in the calculation of each factor score. In addition, within a set of several variables, there may be several different factors, each of which explains some part of the variation in the original variables.

A factor analysis proceeds by examining the patterns of correlations among the variables and identifies those variables that could be used to form factors. These factors are calculated through the use of factor scoring equations similar to those listed below:

$$FS_1 = .40\ A17 + .30\ A18 + .01\ A19 + .05\ A20 + .02\ A21$$

$$FS_2 = .06\ A17 + .03\ A18 + .01\ A19 + .37\ A20 + .51\ A21$$

$$FS_3 = .02\ A17 + .04\ A18 + .55\ A19 + .03\ A20 + .02\ A21$$

To calculate the score on Factor 1, the value of variable A17 (a rating between 1 and 5) would be multiplied by .40 (the factor scoring coefficient for A17 on the first factor), the rating of A18 multiplied by .30, the rating of A19 by .01, and so on. Then the resulting values are added together to form an overall composite score on the first factor. Using the same rating values but a different set of weights, the scores for Factor 2 and Factor 3 are then calculated.

As a result, the factor analysis would have summarized much of the information contained in the five variables (A17 to A21) into the three summary measures (FS_1, FS_2, and FS_3). In large data sets containing, for example, twenty variables, factor analysis may be extremely useful in summarizing the large number of variables into a small number of factor scores.

The following SAS **PROC** would perform a factor analysis with VARIMAX rotation of variables A17 through A21, and would extract three factors:

```
PROC FACTOR DATA=CLEANERS ROTATE=VARIMAX NFACTORS=3;
     VAR A17--A21;
```

SPSS Procedure:

```
FACTOR  VARIABLES = A17 TO A21/ROTATION =  VARIMAX/
        CRITERIA = FACTORS (3)
```

The most relevant portions of the SAS output from a factor analysis are:

The Eigenvalues - These indicate the part of the variation in the data set explained by each factor.

The Factor Loadings - These tell us which variables are most closely associated with each factor.

The Factor Scoring Coefficients - These are the weights illustrated by the above example that allow for the calculation of a set of factor scores for each respondent.

The Factor Scores - These are summary measures produced from the values of the original variables in the data set.

Your marketing research textbook will provide you with a discussion of how to interpret each of these parts of the output and the SAS statistics manual will provide a number of additional options.

ANALYSIS OF VARIANCE

Analysis of variance is a technique for analyzing experimental data. The results of an experiment are usually measured by a numerical response variable, referred to as the criterion variable. This criterion variable is measured under a number of different conditions, identified by one or more classification variables.

Suppose that we had performed an experiment to test two versions of a product that we will call Flavor A and Flavor B. We also believe that there may be differences in taste preferences between males and females. Thus, flavor and sex are the classification variables. We perform our experiment by recruiting a group of eighty subjects (half male and half female) and assigning twenty of them to each of the four experimental treatments in Table 10.1:

TABLE 10.1
EXPERIMENTAL DESIGN FOR FLAVOR EXPERIMENT

Sex/Flavor	Flavor A	Flavor B
Male	20 subjects	20 subjects
Female	20 subjects	20 subjects

In our experimental design, each subject is asked to taste the product and assign a rating on a scale from 1 to 100. Thus, in addition to the two classification variables (sex of respondent and flavor tested, each with two levels), we also have a criterion variable (the score). Our data set may be entered as a line of data for each subject using three variables, A, B, and C, coded as follows:

A	=	a three digit number of the actual scale value assigned.
B	=	Code 1 if male, Code 2 if female
C	=	Code 1 for flavor A, Code 2 for flavor B

The following SAS **PROC** would perform an analysis of variance to test the main effects of

B and C on the criterion variable A, as well as the interaction effect of the combination of B and C:

```
PROC ANOVA DATA=CLEANERS;
     CLASS B C;
     MODEL A  = B C B*C;
     MEANS B C B*C;
```

```
SPSS Procedure:

     ANOVA A BY B(1,2) C(1,2)
     STATISTICS 3
```

The MEANS statement in the above SAS **PROC** would produce the average value of the variable A for each category (level) of B and C, as well as each combination of variables B and C.

CHAPTER ELEVEN
OTHER RESEARCH METHODOLOGIES

We have focused on a specific type of market research study in this project manual. The skills you acquired in completing your project, however, may be generalized to a variety of other types of marketing research. Chapter Eleven briefly presents some of the other commonly used marketing research methodologies and describes their relationship to the type of survey research study described in this manual.

EXPLORATORY RESEARCH

Two types of exploratory studies were mentioned in earlier chapters: focus group interviews and depth interviews. Both of these techniques have the goal of generating insights and ideas regarding marketing problems. They are often used prior to designing descriptive research studies, such as the Apex Dry Cleaners project. Perhaps now you can see how exploratory research, performed prior to conducting your study, might have helped you in:

1. Understanding how consumers think or feel about the product or service of interest.

2. Identifying additional product or service characteristics that could have been evaluated using attitude scales.

3. Generating additional alternatives that could have been evaluated in your study.

Many steps completed in a survey research project such as yours will also have to be done in conducting a focus group or depth interview. Both types of exploratory studies require a sample. They are most likely to rely on judgment samples, in order to ensure that the data gathering will be more productive. These samples might not necessarily be selected directly from the target market. For example, in a study to aid in the design of disposable diapers, we might conduct a focus group among mothers who have already had children, rather than on prospective mothers who will have children in the future. The judgment of the researcher regarding sample selection will be reflected in a screening questionnaire, administered through a small telephone or mall intercept survey to recruit focus group members.

Focus Group Interviewing. The focus group is the most widely used exploratory research technique. The primary data gathering instrument in a focus group is the discussion guide used by the moderator outlining the general areas into which the discussion will be directed. Usually, however, a brief questionnaire similar to the last part of the Apex questionnaire, will be used to learn something about the descriptive characteristics and purchasing habits of the individual participants. If the questionnaire contains questions that could bias the respondents, they are administered at the completion of the group discussion.

Depth Interviews. A research method which often has goals similar to those of the focus group interviewing is depth interviewing. Depth interviews utilize lengthy questionnaires administered by highly skilled interviewers. Other than for the descriptive data, most of the questions contained in a depth interview will be open-ended. Interviewers are trained to probe fully and deeply to get meaningful responses to each question. It is not uncommon for depth interviews to last an hour or longer.

Depth interview sample sizes are usually small, from fifty to hundred responses. However, a large amount of subjective data is generated and its analysis can present a challenge. This requires considerable judgment and intuition to interpret the meaning of the written responses. Focus groups and depth interviews are often analyzed by using content analysis, which resembles a more sophisticated version of coding open-ended questions described in Chapter Seven. Content analysis is often performed twice, by two individuals, as a check on the validity of the interpretation. Suggested procedures for performing content analysis are provided in your marketing research text.

DESCRIPTIVE RESEARCH

A wide variety of marketing research studies fall under the heading of descriptive research. The purpose of a descriptive study is to carefully describe some phenomenon of interest in objective terms. Your research project is an example of a descriptive research study in that your goal was to measure the attitudes, behavior, and descriptive characteristics of a carefully defined group of consumers. Your study was objective because the results were presented in the form of numerical tables which provide an opportunity for meaningful comparison. In this section, we will describe some of the other commonly used descriptive research methods. These and other types of descriptive research are treated in more detail in your marketing research textbook.

Marketing Component Studies. Marketing component studies are designed to perform a detailed exploration of some aspect of the marketing strategy, usually through a survey research method. Marketing component studies could focus on the product itself, its packaging or labeling, its pricing, the distribution preferences consumers, advertising, or personal selling strategy. The key difference between a component study and a segmentation study is the level of detail provided in a specific area. For example, in a segmentation study, we could ask the consumer about the price paid for the product. In a component study focusing on price, we could be interested in a variety of price issues, including but not limited to:

1. The price paid.
2. The expected price.
3. Expected price ranges for products in the category.
4. The relationship between price and expected quality.
5. The use of special prices (e.g., the use of special sales and deals).
6. The effect of price changes on brand loyalty and brand switching.

The higher level of detail implied by the example above could be applied to any area of marketing strategy. In addition to detailed questioning in the specific strategy area, descriptive data would also be included in the questionnaire. The experience you gained in performing your project should be useful to you in executing a product component study.

Tracking Studies. Tracking studies are used to monitor the progress of marketing strategy in one or more areas. Thus, they are longitudinal, implying multiple waves of data gathering conducted at different points in time. Tracking studies are nearly always used in conjunction with a test market of a new product or during the execution of a new advertising campaign. They may also be used once the product is established in order to monitor marketplace performance on a regular basis.

Excellent research design is of particular importance in a tracking study. Research methodology must be carefully prepared prior to executing the first wave of tracking because the primary purpose of the tracking study is to monitor change in various measures of market response. If the research methodology were changed after the tracking study is begun, it may be impossible to determine whether observed changes reflect real changes in the marketplace or simply the change in the research methodology. For example, if two waves of tracking were conducted in a mall intercept interview and then another wave were conducted through a telephone survey, variations in the measures could be caused either by a change in consumer response to the marketing strategy or because the samples are not comparable.

Tracking studies performed during a test market or during the rollout of a new frequently purchased consumer product will focus on at least four areas: brand awareness, brand trial, repeat purchase, and brand loyalty. These measures reflect the hierarchical notion of consumer response suggested in Chapter Four. In addition, attitude measures using semantic differential or Likert scales, will usually be obtained.

Tracking studies may provide considerable diagnostic information regarding poor performance of the new product. For example, suppose that three months after beginning a test market, the manager concludes that brand sales are below expectations. A tracking study might reveal that awareness of the new brand is below expected levels. This could be caused by an insufficient level of advertising, a failure to efficiently direct funds to the target market, or poor advertising quality. On the other hand, if awareness is high, it is possible that the product concept being communicated by the advertising is not sufficiently attractive to generate trial behavior. If trial behavior is at an acceptable level, it could be that consumers are not continuing to buy the product, suggesting that the product may not be fulfilling expectations created by the advertising. Detailed measures of consumer attitudes regarding specific product characteristics could offer explanations for failure in any of the areas of awareness, trial, or repeat purchasing.

The first wave of a tracking study is often conducted prior to the commencement of the test market, product launch, or advertising campaign to provide baseline values of the measures of interest. Subsequent waves are usually timed to coincide with the length of the purchase cycle (the average amount of time between consecutive purchases of a brand by an average consumer).

Conjoint Analysis. A marketing research technique that is very popular with designers of new products is conjoint analysis. A major objective of conjoint analysis is to estimate the relative contribution of different product characteristics to overall consumer preference for the products. However, rather than measuring the rating and importance of each product characteristic (as you may have done in the product-positioning part of your project) conjoint analysis presents consumers with (usually) hypothetical product combinations. These hypothetical products may be presented in the form of sort-cards, each of which will list a particular combination of the product characteristics under study. Below is an example of a sort-card:

TIRE A

50,000 MILE WEAROUT GUARANTEE
PRICE $60
TRACTION RATING - B
RAISED WHITE LETTERS

Respondents are given a deck of sort-cards, each presenting a different combination of product characteristics, and are asked to indicate their relative preference for each product combination by ranking the concepts from most preferred to least preferred. The data resulting from a conjoint analysis task will be a set of preference rankings for the various combinations of product characteristics. This data is usually analyzed using a technique called monotonic regression. The result of the analysis is a set of estimated utilities, numbers that reflect the contribution to preference of each of the product characteristics. Using a knowledge of these utilities, the product designer can develop new product concepts encompassing various product characteristics. The level of preference consumers are likely to have for each of these products may be predicted from a knowledge of the utility of each characteristic.

CAUSAL RESEARCH

Neither exploratory nor descriptive research studies are capable of accurately predicting the likely outcome of alternative marketing strategies. Causal research methods are used specifically for this purpose. The terms *causal research* and *experimentation* are occasionally used as though they were one and the same. In fact, many types of causal research could not, technically, be called experiments. A true experiment implies a high degree of researcher control over all sources of variation as well as the random assignment of subjects being exposed to the things being tested.

It would be more appropriate to associate the term *causal research* with different types of testing, whether the tests are experimental or nonexperimental. Many types of causal research are used by marketing managers to test the expected consequences of various alternatives. These include concept testing, advertising copy testing, and product testing.

Concept Testing. Concept testing is used primarily in the early design stages of the new product planning process to predict consumer reactions to product ideas before substantial funds are invested in their development. Concept tests may also have the goal of improving and refining concepts. Concepts may be presented in many forms varying from brief written sentences to finished advertising copy. In either case, the concept being tested will be a simple statement which describes the concept and indicates its principle benefits. Sometimes, several new ideas will be tested in the same study, and additional concept statements may be used to describe existing products in the product category. These concept statements may be listed on index cards and presented to the consumer singly or in pairs.

A number of measures may be used to evaluate concept tests. The most common measure is intention to purchase (ITP), illustrated by the following scale:

How likely are you to purchase this product if it were available in stores where you typically shop? Do you think you would:

> **definitely buy it.**
> **probably buy it.**
> **might or might not buy it.**
> **probably not buy it.**
> **definitely not buy it.**

The purchase intentions indicated by the ITP question can be refined with an intent translation model that reduces estimated intention to account for the likelihood that intentions will be overstated.

As with most research studies, concept tests share some elements in common with the project you performed. The samples in a concept test are often quite small (as few as fifty respondents). However, some of the sampling methods discussed in Chapter Six could be used to recruit a group of concept-test participants. Except for specific standardized questions regarding purchase intention, the questionnaire may also resemble the questionnaire in your study.

Advertising Copy Testing. Given the tremendous amount of advertising spending by companies, it should not be surprising that advertising testing is a major area of marketing research. *The Journal of Advertising Research* regularly presents articles on new methodologies for advertising testing.

Advertising copy testing may take place at various points throughout the copy development process. Advertisers test rough copy, smooth copy at various stages of development, and the effects of final copy in test markets or market rollouts. A variety of consumer reactions to advertising copy may be tested, including general advertising awareness, brand awareness, brand comprehension, playback of specific copy points, brand attitude, and various measures of the persuasiveness of the advertising. Several different measures will usually be included in a questionnaire, providing the primary basis for the evaluation of the results of the test.

The settings for testing advertising copy also vary widely. Testing of television advertising may be done by inserting advertisements into a typical types of programming such as a made-for-television movies or situation comedies. The programming is then presented to large groups of respondents (e.g., 200 to 300) in movie theaters, some of which are designed specifically for this purpose.

Another method of testing finished television advertising copy that is growing in popularity is on-air testing through cable television systems. The ability to test multiple advertisements simultaneously through split-cable television offers the opportunity to conduct field experiments in a totally natural environment.

Laboratory Testing of Products.   Laboratory testing offers the marketing researcher the capability of conducting true experiments in a controlled environment.   In a laboratory setting, subjects can be randomly assigned to the various experimental treatments (e.g., different flavors of the product or different packaging methods), and nearly every element that might affect the person's responses to the treatment may be either controlled or at least measured.   The laboratory testing of products usually takes place during the early stages of the product design process, when it is desirable to measure the effect of one or more product variations.   Perhaps the most typical laboratory testing of products is taste testing.

In laboratory experimentation the goal typically is to isolate and measure the effect of some variable that is manipulated by the researcher.   For this reason, laboratory experiments usually offer the most persuasive evidence in favor of a causal relationship between a specific experimental treatment (e.g., a flavor of a product) and a criterion measure (e.g., level of preference for the flavor).

Testing of Products in Natural Environments.   The controlled environment of the laboratory offers the ability to connect specific effects to specific causes.   However, the high level of control over all aspects of the experiment is also a weakness, since the results may not be predictive of the actual behavior of consumers in the marketplace.   Thus, once products have been formulated and prototypes developed, home usage testing is often used to determine consumer reactions to the product under normal conditions.   When the product has been formulated around a well-developed product concept (see the discussion of concept testing above), this method may be used to test concept fulfillment.   Concepts are fulfilled when the benefits promised by the concept are realized by the consumer when actually using the product.   Home usage testing may also be a good predictor of repeat purchasing. Intention to purchase questions (similar to those used in the concept test) are typically asked.   However, the value of the two tests (concept versus product) is different. In the concept test, we are trying to determine if the concept is sufficiently attractive to persuade the consumer to try the product.   In the home usage situation, however, the consumer has actually had a chance to try the product and is now being asked about the desirability of using it again.